"A no-nonsense guide to thinking and behaving more flexibly in order to have a happier, better, less frenetic life."
   —*Marie Claire*

"Using case studies and Annie's own experience as the cofounder of cultural insight agency Starling, *Flex* is full of motivation to challenge the status quo and reshape the routines and social norms women are confined by."
   —*The Sunday Times Style*

"Women face more of an uphill battle with extra pressure to be perfect at home and work. Auerbach offers solutions in her book *Flex*."
   —*The Sun*

"Straight-talking self-help. . . . Inspiring words, practical help, and a fresh way of seeing things that we'll be forcing on just about everyone we know."
   —*Stylist*

"*Flex* is an intelligent and playful manifesto for happier living in a world of distraction and overload. Thought-provoking, wise, funny, and packed with surprising ideas that are genuinely useful. Highly recommended."
   —**Dr. Mark Williamson, director of Action for Happiness**

"Annie is such a hugely influential voice in the push toward a working world that looks at what people are doing, not where they are sitting. For anyone truly wanting to implement flexible working, this is a must read."
   —**Anna Whitehouse, founder of *Mother Pukka***

FLEX

FLEX

Reinventing Work
for a Smarter,
Happier Life

Annie Auerbach

HarperOne
An Imprint of HarperCollins*Publishers*

HarperCollins books may be purchased for educational, business, or sales promotional use. For information, please email the Special Markets Department at SPsales@harpercollins.com.

Originally published as *Flex* in Great Britain in 2019 by HQ, an imprint of HarperCollins Publishers, Ltd.

FIRST HARPERCOLLINS PAPERBACK EDITION PUBLISHED IN 2022

Design adapted from the *Flex* edition designed by Louise Evans.

Library of Congress Cataloging-in-Publication Data is available upon request.

ISBN 978-0-06-305965-8

22 23 24 25 26   LSC   10 9 8 7 6 5 4 3 2 1

TO DARLING CLEMMY,
BIBI & BEN

CONTENTS

FLEX IN FLUX

When I first wrote this book in 2019, I was passionate about flex—flexibility in the workplace and beyond—because I believed the old structures of nine-to-five were harming our ability to live the lives to which we aspired. As I write this, we are living through the COVID-19 pandemic. I hope that by the time you read it, the situation will be calmer. Millions of us all around the world swapped workplaces for makeshift home offices, classrooms for kitchens, office buzz for Zoom fatigue, and rigid hours for a murky blur of life, work, and 24/7 news addiction. When we weren't itching to escape our four walls, we were paralyzed with anxiety. For others, working from home was not an option. They were on the front line delivering food, caring for the vulnerable, and tending to the sick in hospitals overwhelmed with the terrible impact of the virus. All of us struggled to find our feet at a time when our worlds had been rocked. We tried to make sense of it, using phrases like "unprecedented times" and "the new normal."

Yet, there was nothing normal about this period. The flip from business-as-usual to lockdown happened at blistering speed. We were, and still are, truly in flux. The companies that insisted flex could never work scrambled to make it a reality. Those barriers they claimed were insurmountable melted away in the face of a bigger imperative to keep their people safe. Even during such impossibly sad times, it was a poignant thing to witness—the mass adoption of ideas that flexible work pioneers have championed for decades. They had the courage to imagine a different way, and COVID-19—in all its chaos—tipped their vision into the mainstream.

In this book, you'll read their stories and become inspired by their ambition. The ideas behind flex have been bubbling up for decades as the shape of the modern family shifts, retirement age increases, the climate emergency escalates, and technology opens up new possibilities for knowing ourselves and our potential.

The thing is, flex is so much more than a reflex to a crisis. It is bigger than the survival instinct of businesses facing uncertainty. Flex is about a better future with solidarity and diversity at its heart. It welcomes those who might be excluded from a macho working culture of long hours and presenteeism. It values their contributions precisely because they are not the status quo, and therefore their perspectives are bound to be fresh, innovative, and creative.

Flex is not just an interim solution to a workforce on lockdown. It leans into longer, more meandering career paths beset with uncertainty, which require us to learn, relearn, adapt our skills, and pivot. It is an investment in health, rest, and recuperation. A belief that family, friendships, and fun must coexist with hard work rather than be sacrificed at its altar. Flex is about a sustainable approach to living and working.

Flex allows us to shed the stuff that doesn't work for us and the rhythms that don't suit us. The slog of the daily commute has come under scrutiny as we have questioned the sanity of mass synchronized travel on overloaded and unhygienic transport systems for no apparent benefit. We are gaining freedom to listen to our circadian rhythms and mold our days accordingly.

Flex refuses to swap the nine-to-five for the 24/7. We learned during the lockdown that it is hard to compartmentalize work when it is happening on the kitchen table, in bed, or on the sofa. But flex needs to have hard edges, boundaries, and regimes to ensure we don't slip back into old habits and truly benefit from our moment of pause.

Because during the biggest global experiment ever in remote working and learning, we were forced to press the pause button. While it was frustrating, it was also a gift. Our working culture up until then had fetishized speed, churn, and efficiency and neglected empathy, listening, and considered thought. Living through a pandemic meant we all did more of the latter. Recovery will be a long process. When it happens, we can be intentional about the kind of world to which we want to return. We can build a more intelligent, sustainable, and compassionate way of working and living.

This is a moment of reinvention, a chance to move away from the old mindsets laden with rigidity, presenteeism, burnout, and stress. "You never change things by fighting the existing reality," said Buckminster Fuller, American inventor and futurist. "To change something, build a new model that makes the existing model obsolete."

So this is our opportunity to invent the whole thing from scratch. Work culture has been broken. Let's not use old metrics to measure new circumstances. Now is the time to dream up a beautiful new model that makes the old one obsolete.

FLEX

THIS

~

IS

~

FLEX

Flex is a manifesto for living and working on your terms. It means looking at the established, rigid ways of doing things and asking: "Is this really working for me?" If the answer to that question is "No," then read on, because this book is for you.

When we learn how to flex, we gain a superpower that allows us to challenge what is holding us back and to reinvent the rules for a smarter, happier life. Things are changing for women across the globe. We are getting married and having children later, if at all. Dual-income families have replaced the traditional template of man as breadwinner and woman as homemaker. Technology allows us to work differently and understand ourselves better.

But the old systems still persist. We're continually bashing up against inflexible structures that were built by, and for, men. We are trying to do everything while following a rule book we didn't write.

Cartoons of working women depict us as harassed multitaskers with eight octopus arms, juggling food, lipstick, laptop, and wine. Who actually wants to live their lives like this? Who wants to be a jittery octopus lady constantly time-pressed and on the verge of meltdown? Not me.

I've been thinking about flex for a long time. I've worked flexibly for 20 years in many different guises—part-time, remote working, through a portfolio career, and freelancing. I am now 42, I run my own business, and

I have two daughters under 10, a husband, and a small snappy dog—so I am right in the eye of the storm.

In 2016, I founded a cultural insight agency called Starling with my business partner, Adam. At Starling, we help brands understand how society is changing, so they can be more relevant. We speak to the smartest academics and the most radical thinkers. We ask "Why?"; we listen for what's being ignored; we help our clients build better futures. And so I decided to use this approach to look at the old structures that are restricting us and come up with shiny new solutions. Researching how women are working and living today turned out to be an awakening for me.

I have encountered a huge number of people who have found different ways to flex. These pioneers of flexible working may have initially been motivated by the need to manage childcare and responsibilities at home as well as progressing in their careers, but they are also unrecognized revolutionaries who have been chipping away at the systems that society has outgrown. They refuse to accept the status quo, they challenge handed-down wisdom, and they change the game for the rest of us. Quite simply, they are phenomenal, and we need to learn from them. In each chapter, I've featured a story from one of these pioneering flexers.

I wrote this book because I'm inspired by them, and I think the image of stressed, juggling womanhood is past its sell-by date. I don't want to join the army of exhausted octopus women, desperately hashtagging #wineoclock and marching under the banner of "having it all." I don't want to be told I have to be good at everything, all of the time: friendship, leadership, parenting, Pilates, makeup, public speaking, cake baking, even tennis. It's exhausting, it's not cool, and I'm over it.

More and more businesses in different sectors are recognizing the fundamental importance of creativity in their employees, whatever their role, yet we seem to be funneling ourselves into tighter and more restrictive routines and thinking patterns. When we prioritize the wrong things—like long working hours over friendships, exams over mental agility, climbing the established career ladder over cutting our own paths—we diminish and inhibit ourselves and our possibilities. Similarly, when we ignore our bodies' moods and cycles, going against the grain of how we feel or what we really want, then we can only really feel like we're failing, living half-lives.

Flex is a creative, rebellious, badass way to live because it means looking at routines like the nine-to-five and social norms like women bearing the brunt of the emotional load at home, and bending and reshaping them. When you flex, you invent your own template, according to your own ambitions and your family's needs, often without precedent on a truly blank slate.

So to flex we need to be brave. We need to take a long look within and ask, "How can I work to the best of my abilities at work, while being the mother or partner or friend I want to be at home?" And once we've figured out what exactly flex means for us as individuals, we have to find the confidence to go out there and ask for it. Even when it goes against our current climate of pointless meetings, presenteeism, the strictures of nine-to-five, and even society's expectations on us as women. And I want to show you how. The five chapters of this book ask what the concept of flex looks like through different lenses: work, yes, but also our minds, our homes, our bodies, and finally our futures.

We know that the world is changing fast. Rigidity in a world of change means something is going to break, and that something could be you. And think about it: many of the jobs we were trained for in school won't exist in a decade. The more robotic our behavior, the more vulnerable we are to the robots taking our place. So flex has to be, for all of us, a movement built on creativity, bravery, anti-convention, and innovation.

When we learn to flex,
we reinvent the rules for
a new future, and it's one
in which we can all thrive.

FLEX

YOUR

MIND

My day job is coming up with fresh thinking and new ideas for brands. I love ideas. I love the first sniff of one, the gut feeling we're onto something. The hunt for more evidence and the inevitable period of doubt and being "lost in the forest." The joy of getting it down on paper. I love all of it.

Flex is about inventing new answers to old problems and picking at the threads of handed-down wisdom to see what unravels. It means having a low boredom threshold for the "same old, same old." It makes us challenge the status quo and ask difficult questions, like: Is this the way we should be living and working? Are the norms we've all bought into making us happy? This is the opposite of dogma and rigidity. It is a sort of cognitive yoga, an exercise for the mind that stretches our horizons and challenges our biases. It requires bravery, leaps of faith, and empathy. And, annoyingly, it's not easy . . .

SKILL OF THE FUTURE

The World Economic Forum predicts that creativity is one of the top three skills workers will need in the future. The other two are complex problem-solving and critical thinking. The more we flex our creativity muscles, they say, the more we future-proof our skills.

Some days at work, my partner Adam and I are creative ninjas. Other days, we talk about last night's TV shows and what we're going to have for lunch. Creativity isn't effortless, there's no app for it, but it's vital if we are to find new and exciting ways to change the things that are restricting us. In this chapter, I'll dig into the key ingredients for creativity, so that we can unlock it in ourselves. I will look at how our environments have conspired against us to make us inflexible, and I'll show how we can foster the right conditions for creativity to thrive.

Today, whether you're a coffee barista or a CEO, everyone hungers to be creative. The *New Yorker* dubs it "Creativity Creep," saying: "Few qualities are more sought after, few skills more envied. Everyone wants to be more creative—how else, we think, can we become fully realized people?" [1]

Part of this is because we have more time to spend on being creative. As Walter Pitkin observed back in 1932, thanks to medical breakthroughs and time-saving devices like washing machines, "men and women alike turn from the ancient task of *making a living* to the strange new task of *living*." And *living* these days is a creative endeavor. Social media has fetishized visually beautiful lives. Even if we're making a packed lunch for our children, it's got to be inventive, stylish, Instagrammable.

Instagram is full of creativity quotes from smart people. "Creativity is not a talent. It is a way of operating." "Creativity is intelligence having fun!" "You can mimic a result. But not the creativity." These all sound nice and inspiring. You can imagine the fist pumps, the head nods.

But what does creative thinking actually mean?

EVOLUTION & DAD JOKES:
WHAT IS CREATIVITY?

I want to start by looking at a classic case of creativity, a leap in thinking that forever changed the conversation for humankind: the theory of evolution. The fascinating thing about this idea is that it occurred to two different people, Charles Darwin and Alfred Russel Wallace, independently. For two separate thinkers to reach the same idea at the same time is a real rarity.

So what did they do in order to get to their big idea? In an essay published in 1959, American sci-fi writer Isaac Asimov looked at what their creative processes had in common to try to find the key to creativity.[2]

First, they traveled. Darwin took a five-year, round-the-world trip aboard HMS *Beagle* in 1831. Wallace went to the Amazon and Rio Negro basins in 1848, and then, in 1854, to the Malay Archipelago.

Second, both observed unfamiliar species of plants and animals and how they varied from place to place. Darwin famously went to the Galápagos Islands to study finches, tortoises, and mockingbirds. During his travels in what is modern-day Indonesia, Wallace collected more than 100,000 insect, bird, and animal specimens, which he donated to British museums.

Third, both read Thomas Malthus's *An Essay on the Principle of Population*, which predicted that the human population would grow faster than its ability to feed itself. This proved to unlock the puzzle for both men. Reading about overpopulation in human beings sparked their ideas on evolution by natural selection. That's how Wallace and Darwin made their creative leap: by connecting two seemingly unconnected concepts.

Cross-connection may be the key to creativity. The *Oxford English Dictionary* definition of creativity is "the use of imagination or original ideas to create something," but this seems like quite a stretch. Is there really such a thing as pure originality, an idea that has never been thought of before? But smashing together two existing ideas that have never been connected—that is a breakthrough. That is what makes creative friction and sparks something fresh.

"Smashing together two existing ideas that have never been connected—that is a breakthrough.

That is what makes creative friction and sparks something fresh."

As the psychologist Steven Pinker has observed, that is how jokes work. In his book *The Act of Creation*, Arthur Koestler says we laugh when one idea, or frame of reference, sits next to a second one that doesn't initially seem to make sense in the context of the first. So here's a joke: Lady Astor supposedly said to Winston Churchill, "If you were my husband, I'd put poison in your tea." He replied, "If you were my wife, I'd drink it."

Why is this funny? Well, clearly no one wants to be murdered. But when we gear-shift to suicide as a welcome escape from poor old Lady Astor, it becomes funny.

This smashing together of two unexpected frames, where the latter is surprising and causes you to reconsider the former, is called a paraprosdokian (from the Greek "against expectation"). Paraprosdokians are what the rest of us might call "dad jokes." Like Stephen Colbert's "If I am reading this graph correctly—I'd be very surprised." And Groucho Marx's "I've had a perfectly wonderful evening, but this wasn't it."

Koestler's *The Act of Creation* looks beyond comedy to art and science. Creativity in these disciplines, he thought, is also about exploring the relationship between two unrelated ideas. He calls this "bisociation."

For him, creativity is the bisociation of two self-contained but incompatible frames of reference. In short, a dad joke.

IT'S HARDER THAN EVER TO BE CREATIVE TODAY

But it is not as simple as that. We've become really bad at bisociation. Creativity may be higher on the cultural agenda, and it might be a key skill for the future, but the truth is, it is now harder to be creative.

Why is this so? Today, we simply don't have enough bandwidth to be creative. Our technology both overwhelms and distracts us. Every 24 hours people are bombarded with the equivalent of 34 gigabytes of information—that amount would overload a laptop within a week.[3] We can't calmly absorb all this information and metabolize it into beautiful creative thought.

Digital overload is making us act like Dug, the talking dog in Pixar's movie *Up*. Every few moments he interrupts himself mid-speech, ears pricked, nose quivering, and shouts, "SQUIRREL!" Dug is all of us, except our squirrels are tweet storms; siren calls from abandoned, half-filled online shopping carts; the jerk of the leash when we are tagged in a photo.

So we're too distracted to be creative. But even if we manage to focus, our own creativity—our ability to bisociate—is under threat from algorithms. When Amazon nudges us to buy a similar book to the one we've just clicked on, when Netflix cues up yet another

THE STATE OF PERMA-DISTRACTION

Gloria Mark studies digital distraction at the University of California, Irvine. She has found that it takes about 23 minutes to return to the original task after an interruption. So that quick minute spent on Twitter or Facebook isn't just 60 seconds. It's 24 minutes down the drain.[4]

film "with a strong female lead," when social media echo chambers only feed us news that is palatable to us, we're being pigeonholed. We're being funneled down a narrow path. Instead of the quirky, interesting people we imagine ourselves to be, we're becoming self-fulfilling prophecies, living in a bland monoculture. All of this amounts to a navel-gazing outlook (or in-look) that keeps us thinking in the ways we have always thought. We are stuck in a monotonous spin cycle of our own experience, which is a profoundly uncreative place to be.

"Everyone thinks they are right all the time about everything," innovation strategist Faris Yakob told me. "We can't see anyone else's point of view with clarity. We assume they are idiots and racists. It's got to the point where I can't emotionally understand a position that is different from mine. I tend to like reading books about history and politics, but I'm forcing myself to read more fiction. Reading fiction helps you develop empathy and understand better where people you disagree with are coming from."

We also bristle at any opinion that differs from our own. Ian Martin, writer on the British political comedy TV series *The Thick of It*, called Twitter a "shrieking tunnel of fuck." In the midst of this polarized battleground it is harder than ever to find common ground, to flex our positions and move forward. Without respect for another's perspectives or empathy for their experiences, we can't make connections, bisociate, and progress our thinking. Remember, the dictionary definition tells us creativity is "the use of imagination or original ideas to create something." Ouch. Cultural zombies can't be creative, can they? Shrieking trolls won't open their imagination, will they? How can we escape our "tunnel of fuck" and find the fuel for empathy and inventiveness?

STEREOTYPING + CREATIVITY

Evidence suggests that lack of empathy for others is indeed a block to creativity. A 2012 study by Tel Aviv University found that people who "believe that racial groups have fixed underlying essences" did not do as well in creative tests as those who saw racial categories as "arbitrary and malleable." So those who pigeonhole racial groups have "a habitual closed-mindedness that . . . hampers creativity," the study authors wrote.[5]

BECOMING
T-SHAPED

The creative industries are always on the hunt for what they call "T-shaped" people. The vertical bit of the T—the I—is depth of experience in a specific subject. The horizontal bit of the T is a broader range of experience across subjects, which encompasses the capacity to peek over the top of parapets, to collaborate, to find links between different disciplines. Essentially, the horizontal bit of the T is the knack for Koestler's bisociation. So this magical T-shaped human combines the vertical skill of rigor and the horizontal skill of empathy.

But it's really hard to be T-shaped these days. The vertical is being fueled, meaning we are being made more I-shaped by the algorithms that feed us more and more of what we already know. But the horizontal—empathy—needs our active attention. Cross-pollination requires us to break out of our echo chambers, broaden our horizons, and open our hearts and minds to the new.

"Notice things, be curious, talk to people, figure out new ways of doing things."

Travel is one way to do this. Remember both Darwin and Wallace were committed explorers. Faris Yakob and his wife, Rosie, are nomadic creatives who travel around the world working for their consultancy Genius Steals. Travel is very important to them. Faris told me: "Habituation makes you blind. It turns your brain off." Rosie says travel turns it back on again. "There's a discomfort to being in new places," she explains. "It means you need to notice and be curious. The more you travel and the stranger the situations you are in, the more likely you are to expand your surface area and serendipitous things might happen."

It's not enough to simply go on holiday. Two weeks on a sun lounger in Majorca won't cut the creative mustard. You have to do what Rosie talked about: notice things, be curious, talk to people, figure out new ways of doing things.

Not all of us can afford the luxury of traveling in order to boost creativity, of course. But many of us can at the very least get out of the workplace and go for a walk. Research from Creative Equals, an organization that champions diversity in the creative industries, shows that just 9 percent of people have their best ideas while at the office. Fans of the walking meeting include Arianna Huffington, Mark Zuckerberg, and Barack Obama.

The first reason to go for a walk is that we need to move more. We're living in sedentary times, sitting, on average, for 9.3 hours per day—longer than we are sleeping.[6] The second reason is to boost our creativity. Researchers at Stanford University asked people to think up new uses for common objects while sitting at a desk or walking. Over three-quarters came up with more ideas while walking than while sitting.[7]

At Starling, Adam and I walk to client meetings rather than taking the subway. It means we leave with time to spare and don't rush. We use the journey to discuss the meeting ahead, or just chat. Some of our best ideas and conversations happen on walks—a time that otherwise would be a dead zone of getting from A to B.

Walking is second nature. It doesn't require concentration. It allows the mind to wander. The state of the wandering mind has been shown to be fertile for creative ideas and flashes of insight. When we don't try hard to have an idea, it usually comes to us.

HOW TO BE
T-SHAPED

1. Travel. And if you can't travel, be open to new influences wherever they might be—notice things, be curious, ask why. Take a new route to work or school. This will force you to see things slightly differently and confront you with new inputs.

2. Go for a walk on your own, and let ideas sneak up on you. Or with someone else and talk them through.

3. Take a photo each day. This will nudge you to observe, to look harder at everyday things you may otherwise ignore and find new perspectives.

4. Break your echo chamber. I have scrutinized who I follow on Twitter and my aim now is to follow diverse, challenging voices and avoid the loud, obvious ones.

5. Be empathetic. Try to think flexibly and openly about ideas that feel odd and jarring to you.

6. Clash these ideas together, make connections, join dots. Tell dad jokes.

7. Read books. Fiction, nonfiction, anything. Just keep reading.

8. And read things you wouldn't automatically choose. Take inspiration from Stack. Stack is a subscription service that delivers a different specialist magazine each month, on anything from art to tennis.

9. Be OK with having creative droughts. Don't panic. When this happens, see points 2 and 7.

10. Take the pressure off yourself, be in the moment, don't force it. That's when the magic will happen.

PINNY GRYLLS'S FLEX STORY

*Pinny Grylls is a documentary filmmaker
and children's author*

My worst ideas come from sitting on the internet and researching things. You are at a computer, your eyeballs are staring at the screen, there's a digital wall between you and a real story, which has already been mediated several times. I want to get to a new story, a new perspective, not one already told by someone else.

You need to get off your butt and actually physically meet people. Ordinary day-to-day conversations and events can be doors into new ideas and films. An example of this: I was buying a used car and had to pick it up from Stoke-on-Trent. It was going to be a boring task—collecting the car, signing documents, and whatnot. But I was sitting in this guy's living room, and he told me he works as a hypnotist, specializing in doing past-life regression with traumatized people who work as firefighters. These people had ordinary lives, they were not novelists or professional creatives. Yet, under his care, they pop into another realm and become someone else. They tell stories of being a nineteenth-century farmer committing a murder or a priest in Tibet. I was inspired to make a film about it, and it became a Channel 4 documentary.

I try not to impose a story on the world. The way I work is a collaboration between me and the person who wants their story to be told, who wants it to be witnessed. That's why you need to meet people, to get the magic, the intimacy. You don't get it from a screen. You have to be with them physically.

My tip is to give yourself permission not to work. Go on a road trip to buy that used car. It may be a more interesting day than you thought. Don't force yourself to sit at a screen and come up with ideas. Do the laundry. Read a story to your kid. Do ordinary things, and your brain will go somewhere else. Take pressure off those moments and let "being" in your life be enough. When you take pressure off, that's when you find things.

I was diagnosed with an inch-wide benign brain tumor that was right between my eyes. I had radiation therapy and had to go through screening scans every six months afterward. We took time off work and school and went on a mobile-home family road trip around Europe. We thought, "We don't know what the future is, so we want to do this now." Recently, I had a scan to see whether the radiation had worked. If it hadn't, I needed a dangerous operation to remove the tumor. It had shrunk by 25 percent, I was given the all-clear, and it was like being given my life back.

Until that point, I didn't realize I had been in stasis, not being able to plan anything. But ironically, this had allowed me to be more in the moment and to live! We cram so much into our days; we pressure ourselves. We're a culture that is geared up for quantifiable achievement and status. It's hard to get out of that way of thinking. We need to be patient, to give ourselves permission to dream and not fill every moment of downtime. We need to "be" and believe it doesn't matter if nothing creative comes out of it. It's enough being alive. That is the ultimate creative act.

LIBERTY & RESTRAINT

It's tempting to see creativity as relying on complete freedom and expansiveness. Many have found that the opposite is true. Creativity can thrive when there are restrictions and barriers in place. It is these roadblocks that can force breakthroughs. David Ogilvy, the advertising guru known as the original "Mad Man," once said, "Give me the freedom of a tight brief." What did he mean by this?

Limits give you clarity, focus, and purpose.
They also give you a feeling of safety,
and safety gives you the
confidence to
explore.

BEAUTIFUL CONSTRAINTS

Adam Morgan and Mark Barden's book, *A Beautiful Constraint: How to Transform Your Limitations into Advantages, and Why It's Everyone's Business*, refers to a study of children's playground habits. In a playground in a wide-open field where they could run anywhere, children tended to stay in the middle. When faced with complete freedom, it feels more reassuring to be near the other kids, to keep the status quo. However, if you build a fence around the field, children will explore right to the edge and use the whole space. Ironically, in a contained, safe space, you can roam free.

So think about fences for your creativity. Put in some "beautiful constraints" and you might push yourself beyond the status quo. When Olivia Laing wrote her novel *Crudo*, her "fences" were that she would write every day and she wasn't allowed to go back and edit. She finished it in seven weeks. She said: "Because there was no intention or plan, I wasn't self-conscious and I wasn't worried about trying to get perfect sentences, it was just smashing them down as fast as I could."

If you are a procrastinator, your "fence" could be a strict time limit on the task ahead. If you are the sort of person who makes long lists about what you need to get done, reduce them to one bullet point. This is your creative objective for the day.

Constraints also make you work harder to be creative and push you to excel. Jerry Seinfeld bans himself from jokes containing sex or swearing—it's just too easy to get a laugh. These limits raised his game and upped his comic creativity. He says: "A person who can defend themselves with a gun is just not very interesting. But a person who defends themselves through aikido or tai chi? Very interesting."[8] He treats his stand-up sessions as scientific experiments, analyzing the type and length of laugh he gets for each joke and using that analysis to shave off a word, honing his routine until it is pitch perfect. For him, the creativity lies in what's left out.

If you have creative paralysis, write a list of everything this is NOT. So if, say, you are planning a bachelorette party for a friend, write down everything she would hate first of all. These are your guardrails—and you can create freely within them.

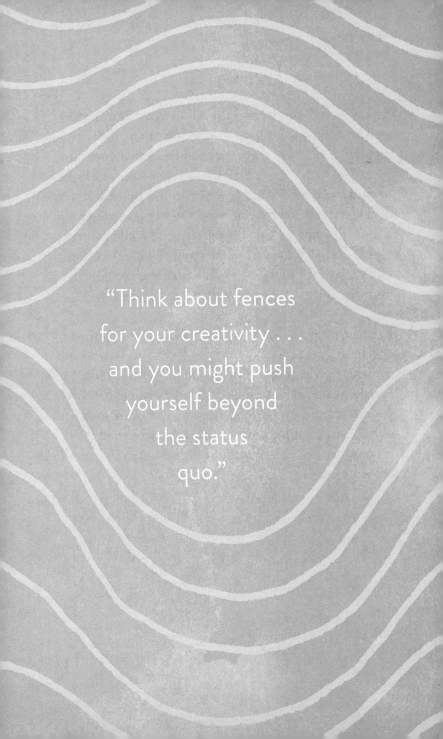

"Think about fences
for your creativity . . .
and you might push
yourself beyond
the status
quo."

Rules can give you freedom from interruption. We've seen how insidious digital distraction can be today, sapping much more real time than the actual diversion took. The writer Zadie Smith has a zero-tolerance policy toward social media and doesn't connect to the internet during her writing time, leaving any fact-checking until she has finished writing for the day. "If I could control myself online, if I wasn't going to go down a Beyoncé Google hole for four and a half hours, this wouldn't be a problem. But that is exactly what I'd do," she says.

Experiment with using airplane mode on your phone and setting strict times of the day (at the beginning and the end) in which to deal with emails. Use apps like Freedom and SelfControl, which allow you to block your own access to websites, apps, or the entire internet to stop wasting time online. Use time before bed to read, rather than being on your phone—stretch your empathy muscles.

Creativity also requires chutzpah. "Chutzpah" is a Yiddish word that refers to self-confidence or bravery. Clashing disciplines, making connections, bisociation: none of this can be done by someone suffering from self-doubt. You needed swagger to say the Earth was round when everyone thought it was flat. You need guts to walk away from accepted wisdom. "The difficulty lies not so much in developing new ideas," said John Maynard Keynes, "as in escaping from old ones."

CHANNEL YOUR CHUTZPAH

Escaping the "old ones" can be hard because they've been handed down to us as gospel. Our parents might have even embedded these ideas in our bedtime stories. And moving away from them makes a statement that you do not need their (or society's) approval anymore.

We can all do this, but what gets in the way is the belief that creativity only lies in the hands of very few select people. The notion that true creatives are artists, misfits at the edges of society, or geniuses who are "ahead of their time" is a barrier to creativity. It lets you say: "Creativity lives in others, but not in me." It stops you from being brave and robs you of your chutzpah.

One of the most generous and powerful speeches on this comes from the Australian comedian Hannah Gadsby. In her game-changing performance *Nanette*, she takes a swipe at the "great men of art" school of thought, which characterizes people like Van Gogh and Picasso as lone, eccentric geniuses.

Gadsby says: "People believe that Van Gogh was just this misunderstood genius, born ahead of his time. What a load of shit. Nobody is born ahead of their time! It's impossible. . . . Artists don't invent zeitgeists, they respond to them. . . . [Van Gogh] was not ahead of his time. He was a post-Impressionist painter painting at the peak of post-Impressionism."

We're all products of our time. We all swim in the cultural soup. Our creativity comes from how we respond to it. Bravery, daring, escaping the old ideas— we can have them all. We just need the chutzpah to do so.

"We all swim in
the cultural soup.
Our creativity comes
from how we
respond to it."

HOW TO CHANNEL YOUR CHUTZPAH

1. Notice the moments when you have been brave in the past. When you owned up to a mistake. Or you called out an injustice. Why did you do it? How did you feel? If you recognize and cherish those moments, you can summon them again when you are in need of chutzpah.

2. Don't feel self-conscious and let it inhibit your ideas. No one is thinking about you. That sounds a bit sad, but it's actually liberating. No one is thinking of you! They are too busy thinking about themselves. Remember Coco Chanel's words: "I don't care what you think about me. I don't think about you at all."

3. Work out who diminishes your bravery. Who is your Achilles heel? Who do you always feel sheepish or inhibited around? These people are drains. Instead, try to hang around people who boost your mojo.

4. Done is better than perfect. Obsessing about perfection is navel-gazing and paralyzing. Get it done, get it out, get on with life.

5. If all else fails, channel Dolly Parton. She said: "Find out who you are. And do it on purpose."

Then dare, shed the old assumptions—and create.

SUMMARY

Modern life is conspiring to make us into cultural zombies. Creativity is scarcer and more urgent than ever. In order to flex, we need to interrogate what we really want and what we need to change to get it—and to do this we must have the space to think creatively. Creativity is a muscle that needs exercising—think of it as cognitive yoga—in order to dodge the algorithmic monoculture that wants to swallow us up.

So when an idea hits you, let it run. Comedian Dave Chappelle says that for him, creativity involves letting go. "If I have an idea, it's the driver. The idea says, 'Get in the car,' and I'm like, 'Where am I going?' The idea says, 'I don't know. Don't worry about it. I'm driving.' Sometimes I'm shotgun, sometimes I'm in the fucking trunk. The idea takes you where it wants to go." [9]

Let your ideas take you where they want to go. Swim in the cultural soup, read books, react to what's out there. Listen to people, meet them face-to-face, empathize with them, look them in the eye, and connect with them. Don't try to be ahead of your time; be of your time and say something different about it.

But most importantly, trust in yourself, be brave, and nourish your own chutzpah. Creativity doesn't live in the hands of lone geniuses. It lives in us all.

FLEX

YOUR

WORK

I was a director at a global research agency. Six months earlier I'd given birth to my second daughter. I had come back to work after maternity leave and negotiated a part-time, three-day-a-week contract. I'd achieved the holy grail: flexibility. I could look after my baby and three-year-old while holding down the job I loved. I should have been triumphant, clicking my heels together as I trotted off into the sunset, swinging a laptop case in one hand and a diaper bag in the other, the clichéd stock image of a working woman.

But, no. It was a disaster. It was one of the most pressure-filled and stressful periods of my life, peppered with moments when I felt I was failing. Here are some examples:

~ When I left work right on time and felt my colleagues' raised eyebrows and disapproval haunt me as I galloped to the subway station.
~ When I arrived sweating, frazzled, and tense to take over from the nanny for the battleground of a toddler bath time.
~ When I sat on the toilet seat and mindlessly chugged a ten-minute Instagram fix.
~ When I worked more, unpaid, than my three allotted days, answering emails on days off and writing reports after I put my daughter to bed.

~ When I frantically tapped out a work email at the edge of the sandpit while my daughter got into fistfights over buckets and spades.

I remember a poignant news story during this period. The number of playground accidents was apparently on the rise. Kids were falling off climbing frames, being flattened by swings, and jettisoned from seesaws. I linked it with the hordes of distracted moms like me, squinting over iPhones on benches at the edges of the playground, trying to reply to incessant requests from colleagues on their days off. My failed flexibility would land my kid in the hospital, I was sure of it.

And even if it didn't, I still felt guilty that those precious two days with my daughter were so un-fun. I was un-fun. I was exhausted, constantly multitasking, never focused on the present, mind swiveling to the next task. I was like one of those terrible people at parties who keep looking over your shoulder in case there's a sexier guest—except I was doing that to my own daughter. And the sexy guest was a boring email about a work meeting. And yet all the time, throughout this period, I felt grateful. Grateful to my bosses for giving me the chance to feel like I was failing in every respect.

I know. Get the violins out. All of this constitutes a "First-World problem." Things were largely OK, and I'm sure my story is no different from any other working parent's. But clearly, flexibility, as I had it, was a shitshow.

I wanted to understand why it was such a fiasco when I tried to flex my working hours around parenthood. And why are we all so wedded to the nine-to-five, five days a week?

I found, as I will show in this chapter, that it's not enough to simply convince your employers to agree to flexibility, as I had done. This is just the beginning. The flexible arrangement actually needs to work, too. And that requires new ways of thinking from both the employer and the employee.

This chapter will look at our modern relationship with time and understand why the nine-to-five (or longer) has become the norm. I will explain what is currently broken within work culture today—the pressures and rigidity that are making people ill, sad, and overwhelmed. I will examine the concept of flexible working that seeks to address work and life, without feeling that we are failing at both. And I will give tips on how to achieve flexible working that works, for everyone. The story begins—let's face it, it often does—in sixteenth-century Italy.

GALILEO, COFFEE BREAKS & SYNCHRONIZED TIME

Galileo Galilei, a 19-year-old student at the University of Pisa, is attending mass at the Duomo di Pisa. The year is 1583. Let's imagine he is bored and his mind is wandering. He's staring at the ceiling when he notices a lamp swinging on a long metal chain. As Steven Johnson explains in *How We Got to Now*, "No matter how long the arc, the lamp seems to take the same amount of time to swing back and forth." Galileo can't test this out by timing it on his watch. Watches don't exist yet, and nor do particularly reliable clocks. So Galileo measures the swing of the lamp against his own pulse. And the idea for a pendulum clock is born.

The pendulum clock changed our relationship with time. Back in the sixteenth century, there were no accurate clocks, but, never having had them, no one really missed them. People weren't racing for trains, rushing home to watch the football game, or dialing into another unnecessary conference call at 1:45 p.m. Everyone was on their own, meandering, unaligned schedule.

Precise synchronized time, as we think of it now, is a modern concept, born out of the Industrial Revolution. Factory work, clocking in and out, taking lunch breaks when instructed to by the boss—all of this built to a sense of coordinated time, with strict divisions between work and leisure. When Welsh social reformer Robert Owen fought for an eight-hour working day in 1817, demanding "eight hours labor, eight hours recreation, eight hours rest," these rhythms became synchronized habits and the modern nine-to-five was born.

That suited an industrial economy. But today, across the world, we are moving from a manufacturing-based economy to a service-based economy. Service-based economies are dominated by tourism, social work, creative industries, retail, and media, among others. Of course, there are some jobs where flexibility is harder to manage—doctors, police officers, call-center workers who need to cover specific hours. But many of us who sit at desks should have more control of our time.

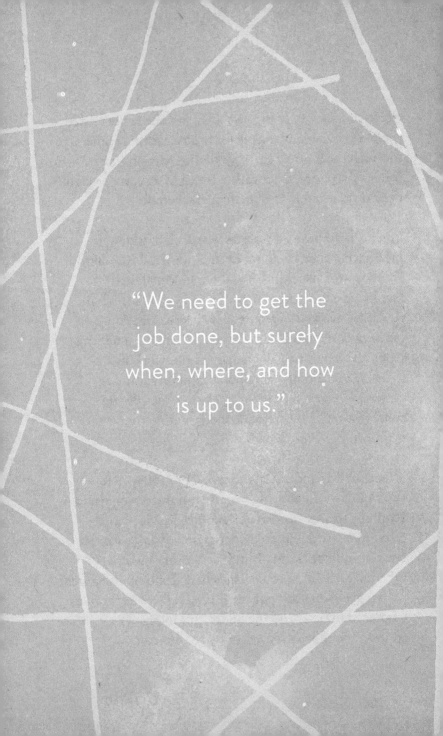

"We need to get the
job done, but surely
when, where, and how
is up to us."

We need to get the job done, but surely when, where, and how is up to us. Yet the hangover of fixed, long hours prevails.

Why is this?

Dale Southerton, professor of sociology of consumption at the University of Bristol, is an expert on time usage. He told me that throughout society there are "traces and resonances of past temporal rhythms." Which is why in England we automatically fancy a cup of tea and a biscuit at 11 a.m., almost as if the factory morning break is imprinted on our collective memories.

Despite having more control over our time in a service-based economy, we slip into the habits and timings of previous generations. Southerton talked of the etymology of the word "routine." It comes from the French *route*, or road. He used the metaphor of a muddy track through a field. Even though we can walk through the field in any direction, we tend to follow the track that previous walkers have left. Throughout society, groups and businesses follow paths, rhythms, and routines that previous generations have established. There's a safety to it: you won't fall down a hole or get lost and you'll avoid hidden snakes in the grass.

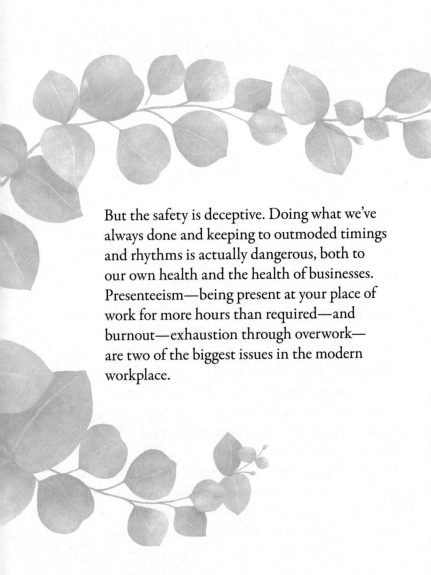

But the safety is deceptive. Doing what we've always done and keeping to outmoded timings and rhythms is actually dangerous, both to our own health and the health of businesses. Presenteeism—being present at your place of work for more hours than required—and burnout—exhaustion through overwork— are two of the biggest issues in the modern workplace.

THE OPPOSITE OF FLEX: BURNED-OUT BUTTS IN SEATS

Today, we're slaves to presenteeism. Being there in body if not in spirit. Long working hours. Working while sick.

The big irony about butts in seats is that these long-suffering butts are proving to be deeply unproductive butts. Working longer hours doesn't always translate into more productivity. Europe is facing a productivity crisis. Productivity in the UK is particularly woeful. The UK's labor productivity, usually measured as the value of goods and services produced for each hour worked, is near the bottom of the G7 league table.

The average French worker produces more by the end of Thursday than their UK equivalent does in a full week. (And that's with the French taking a long lunch and a *cinq à sept* visit to their lover—just kidding.) However, Japan—home of the salaryman, crazy long hours, and *karōshi* (translation: death by overwork)—is even less productive than the UK![10]

A story about this. A Japanese friend, who is a very talented graphic designer, while working for a media firm in Tokyo, once didn't leave his office for two weeks. Two weeks! He popped to the shops to buy some underwear, a toothbrush, and some new shirts. But he ate, slept, and worked in the office for a fortnight. All of his team did. It was expected of them, as they had to meet a deadline, and anyone going home would have been seen as uncommitted, a shirker. By the end of it, they were all zombies, delirious with overwork.

Clearly being present doesn't mean being productive.

PRESENT BUT NOT CORRECT

Eighty-six percent of respondents to a 2018 UK survey said that they had seen presenteeism in their organization, up from 26 percent in 2010.[11] This devotion to butts in seats is costing us dearly: people turning up to work while sick alone leads to a lost productivity cost of just over £4,000 per person each year on average, according to Nottingham Business School research.[12]

And yet leaving work still doesn't mean we relax. Leavism, where people are using holiday time to work, is on the up.[13] Never mind answering emails at the playground; some of us are waking up during the night to do so. One in three Britons are so stressed at work, they have checked their emails in the middle of the night.[14]

Working nine-to-five (and more) is no longer fit for purpose. Unchecked, we're sleepwalking into a global mental health crisis. The Trade Union Congress found that stress brought on by long working hours and lack of job security is the top health and safety concern in workplaces. Our existing work culture in the UK is making us sick. And in Japan, it's actually killing us.

THE CALL FOR FLEX

This is where flexibility comes in. The Equality and Human Rights Commission has issued a call to action: "We need to overhaul our culture and make flexible working the norm."

People desperately want to work flexibly.

It's easy to assume that it's women, and in particular mothers, who crave flex; to be with their children, run the home, or care for their elderly relatives. And yes, it is true that mothers have been at the forefront of pushing for flexibility. But for too long it's been ghettoized, labeled a "mom thing," a women's issue that needs to be solved by women. It's not just mothers that want flexibility. Young people, old people, men and women, they all want it, too.

THE FLEX GAP

There's a gap between the desire to flex and the availability of flexible work. US consultancy Werk .found 96 percent of the workforce needs some form of flexibility, yet only 47 percent have access to a range of flexible options.[15] In the UK, *Marketing Week* found that 87 percent of marketeers want flexibility, yet only 34.2 percent have used flexible working in the last year.[16]

For young people, a good job is a flexible job. They don't envy their burned-out bosses who never see their families. They value having control over when and how they work. Flex even trumps pay for them. A higher salary won't necessarily guarantee loyalty, but flexibility (along with diversity and inclusion) will often inspire commitment from young talent today. This might be because they want a portfolio career, and to make money from different talents on different days of the week. Or they might want to do charity work alongside their main job. They may be hard workers who labor into the night in the hope that their side hustle becomes their main one. They may simply be looking for variety.

"For too long it's been ghettoized, labeled a 'mom thing,' a women's issue that needs to be solved by women."

And those a bit older, the sandwich generation who look after both elderly parents and their own children, want flexibility, too. In the US, 61 percent of those who provide care for an older adult are also balancing jobs.[17] They need to be able to take their parents to the odd doctor's appointment in the middle of the day. Or they need to be with them at the start and end of the day, to take over from caregivers.

Flexibility is crucial to keeping these people—grown-up sons and daughters who care for their parents—in the workforce.

THE HEALTH BENEFITS OF FLEX

A review of ten studies carried out by researchers at Durham University shows mental health, blood pressure, and sleep patterns were better among people who could determine their own working hours.

So all of these diverse groups can benefit practically, physically, and emotionally from flexible working. But this is not just about parents, caregivers, and younger people. Any one of us can also benefit creatively. The staff at 21212, a Michelin-starred restaurant in Edinburgh, are trialing a four-day week (without reducing their salaries) in order to boost the creative flair of the team. They believe the day off will give them the space to find fresh inspiration to bring back to work.

This idea of the four-day work week has been getting more attention recently. Whether the fifth day is spent taking the time for yourself, your hobby, or your family, it is a way of finding space for inputs instead of continual outputs. This can only improve our energy and creativity.

CAN YOU BE
MORE FLEXIBLE?

Flexible working in the broadest sense is a work practice that gives employees flexibility on how long, where, and when they work. But what form of it is right for you?

All employees—not just parents and caregivers—have the legal right to ask for flexible working if they have been in the job for a set period of time. This varies around the world. In the UK it's twenty-six weeks. You should put your request in writing, date it, explain it is a statutory request, and describe what you would like, when you would like it to start, and how that will alter your existing arrangement. You can only make one request in any twelve-month period. Your employer must consider your request seriously, but they can reject it if they believe quality, performance, or standards will suffer or if additional costs are prohibitive. For a full list of reasons why employers might refuse a request, and helpful advice on the process, have a look at the Citizens Advice website.

AMELIA TORODE'S FLEX STORY

*Amelia Torode is the founder of
the Fawnbrake Collective*

I'd spent 20 years in London and New York working for incredible companies like Ogilvy, TBWA, and WPP. As I grew more senior, my role shifted to management and developing strategies for agencies to pursue "digital transformation." I came to a point where I realized that I just didn't believe that "digital transformation" of twentieth-century structures was possible.

I had a lot of time to think about this when I took time out of work to care for my mom, who was battling cancer. By the end, she was really sick and it hurt her to talk, so often we just sat together as she dozed. I thought about the professional world of advertising and branding that I had stepped out of and the frustrations that I'd had about my life. When you are with someone you love who does not have much time left, you start to think about how you spend your time, and I questioned how wisely I was spending mine. There's a wonderful Martin Luther King quote in which he talks about "the fierce urgency of now." I started to feel that urgency very deeply.

I launched the Fawnbrake Collective toward the end of 2017. It's a light-touch collective of entrepreneurial small businesses and independent consultants and creatives, brought together through shared values and ambitions and a belief that we solve and create better together—collaboratively, collectively—than isolated and alone. There are hundreds of Fawnbrakers, but only two full-time employees, myself and Sera Miller, my cofounder. We have a strong element of social enterprise, with pro bono work for charities/not-for-profits woven throughout the commercial model and a commitment to genuine diversity and practical flexibility.

We wanted to get rid of as many structures as we could that we felt were getting in the way of doing the work: so no HQ, no email, no hierarchy, and no bureaucracy. When it came to thinking about talent, we believe it's not about "owning" the people who work for you, but your need to access the best talent. Too much time is spent on professional presenteeism rather than trusting people to work the way that works best for them, so we believe in impact, not hours.

My new working life is time spent smarter. I choose the projects I want to work on, I curate the teams, and I lead by example. I drop the kids off at school, I have started swimming in our local public pool regularly and run daily—things I could never seem to manage to do before. It's not perfect and I don't consider myself a role model, but I am trying to build something new and smarter to live the life that makes me feel challenged, engaged, and balanced.

Here are some different types of flexible working you could think about:

1. **Job sharing:** two people share the work and pay of a single full-time job.

2. **Flexi-hours:** an employee works a set amount of core hours from the office, for example, 10 a.m.–3 p.m. in order to do the school run, and works the remainder of their hours in their own time (for example, after 7 p.m.).

3. **Location-flex:** an employee can work at remote locations either all of the time or some of the time.

4. **One-off flex:** a worker can adapt to unforeseen circumstances (a school concert, a sick mother, even a must-see art exhibition) without being penalized, and make up those hours later.

5. **Flexi-timetabling:** people create their own working timetable that suits their own needs—for example, night owls could work an 11 a.m.–7 p.m. day, or those with awkward commutes could work 7 a.m.–3 p.m. to avoid the rush hour.

6. **Flex-banking:** you work a 4-day week but get paid for a 4.5-day week and that 0.5 is banked. When the business needs you for an extended period, they can give you notice, book you in, and cash in the banked time.

7. **Term-time flex:** full-time work during agreed-upon flexible hours and no work in the holidays.

8. **Compressed hours:** working the equivalent of full-time hours but squashed into fewer days.

9. **Annualized hours:** working a certain number of hours over the year with flexibility about when you work. You could work regular "core hours" and work the rest of your hours flexibly or when there's extra demand at work.

10. **Phased retirement:** older workers can reduce their hours gradually and work part-time before transitioning to full-time retirement.

Well, flexibility sounds fantastic for the workers, but is it actually beneficial for companies and organizations too?

In short, yes it is.

It is great for the culture of a business. A rising tide of evidence shows flexible working practices breed a culture of motivation, engagement, and productivity.[18] Employees with flexibility are more likely to feel their ideas are valued and to believe they work in an environment that fosters diverse points of view.[19] And the good vibes aren't just felt internally. It's great for an employer brand. Employees with access to flexibility are more willing to recommend their workplace to others than those without.

Flexible working can also help with retention. HR departments fear existing mid-level talent will leave if not offered flexibility. Replacing talent is expensive and flex is a reason for people to stay.

Allowing people to work from home cuts costs too: fewer people in the office simultaneously means reduced rent and running costs. It can also impact productivity and profit. At China's biggest travel agency, Ctrip, employees who were "location independent" a few days per week were shown to be more productive than their colleagues who worked exclusively in the office, and resignations among this group fell by 50 percent. And the results showed in the bottom line: the business made about $2,000 more profit per person working from home.[20]

AVOIDING
THE SHITSHOW, OR
MAKING FLEX WORK

Given these clear benefits for both workers and companies, how can we avoid the mess I made of it and get flexibility to work?

At Starling, the cultural insight agency I cofounded in 2016, we interview world experts to help us understand cultural change. One such interview was with Cindy Gallop, sex tech entrepreneur, founder of MakeLoveNotPorn and self-described lover of "blowing shit up." Gallop said something that made me stop and think: "Here's a guaranteed formula for business success. Seek out and recruit the very best talent. Give that talent an inspiring and compelling vision of what you want to achieve. Then stand back. Let them work in any ways they see fit. Demonstrate how much you value and trust them. Give them a high-trust working environment."

Those words, "Let them work in any ways they see fit. Trust them," echoed in my head.

And I realized that, until Starling, I had never worked in a high-trust business culture. One in which I have been trusted to do my job in the way that best made sense to me, without judgment, without fearing it would hinder my chances of progression. And it struck me that without a high-trust culture, it would be near impossible for flexibility to work.

The biggest worry people have about working flexibly is that they will be perceived to be less dedicated. One of my friends told me about a recent job interview. She explained to her potential employer she would like to work one day from home—she lived a 90-minute commute away—so she could pick up the kids from school, and work extra during the time she would save on the commute. They turned her down saying it didn't sound like she was committed to the job.

There is a stigma attached to asking for flexibility. Studies show that many who ask for flex worry they will be penalized as a result—for example, given wage penalties, lower performance evaluations, and fewer promotions. According to a 2016 survey, men don't take extended parental leave because they fear it will jeopardize their position at work.[21] These are all worries about "flexism"—discrimination against flexible workers.

"Without a
high-trust culture,
it would be near
impossible for
flexibility to work."

I had the sense that when I asked for flexibility, I slipped into a slower track at work. The perception of my seniority and experience seemed to ebb away. It didn't feel like I was in the frame for promotion. Part-time working somehow shrouded me in an air of demotion.

People feel stigmatized for asking for flex. But perhaps with good reason, because some employers believe that flexible workers *will* slack off, play the system, and be less productive.

This all shows that there is a deep trust crisis around flexible working. When leaders don't have faith that their workers will keep to their side of the bargain, they don't believe in them. They don't think the flexible working arrangement will succeed and they hand down their suspicions to the rest of the business. The upshot is low trust permeating the whole organization. This is partly to do with the embedded doctrine that a good worker works long hours (wrong on so many levels, as we've seen).

The problem is flexible working isn't "sexy." Stories of successful and productive flexible working need to be told loudly and proudly around the organization. People who are brilliant at what they do, and who are flexing with elegance and excellence, need to become famous at work. This will give managers the confidence to not only say yes to requests but also to really believe in them. And it will give workers who need or want flexibility the reassurance they won't be nudged onto the slow track.

There are other ways in which businesses are actively trying to make flex work. CEO of Pepsi Australia and New Zealand Robbert Rietbroek leads by example. "Leave loudly," he says. "If I occasionally go at 4 p.m. to pick up my daughters, I will make sure I tell the people around me, 'I'm going to pick up my children.' Because if it's OK for the boss, then it's OK for middle management and new hires."

Leaving loudly is a sign that the business respects parenthood, rather than asking its people to leave their parenthood at the door. Too often working fathers and mothers are made to apologize for the fact they are parents. They are seen as the ones who leave early, the flaky ones, the uncommitted.

Annie Crombie, a friend and brilliant CEO in the not-for-profit sector working a four-day week, talks about this. "Most of my madness of working weekends, evenings, and being on my BlackBerry in the playground

YOU'VE GOT MAIL

Another sign that a business is trying to make flex work is its attitude to email. When businesses think intentionally about email and have policies that protect their workers from the onslaught of emails out of working hours and on the weekends, it's a signal they are thinking progressively about flexible working too. French politician Benoît Hamon speaks emphatically about the curse of connectivity for the modern worker: "Employees physically leave the office, but they do not leave their work. They remain attached by a kind of electronic leash—like a dog. The texts, the messages, the emails—they colonize the life of the individual to the point where he or she eventually breaks down."[22] In France, businesses with more than 50 employees are required by law to guarantee workers the "right to disconnect" from technology after they leave the office.

In Germany, Volkswagen has blocked its servers from sending or receiving emails from smartphones between 6:15 p.m. and 7 a.m. on weekdays and weekends.

If companies put in place, and respect, boundaries about email usage and make clear what expectations are in terms of replying on days off, flex has a better chance of working. If they educate the team *around* the flexible worker to buy into these boundaries, for example ensuring they don't bombard them with emails on their days off or arrange important face-to-face meetings when they are working remotely, the system will work all the better for everyone.

on my day off stems from worrying what people think of my competence. There are days when I feel kick-ass and full of self-worth, and these are the days I put my BlackBerry away and push the swing with both hands."

It astounds me she would feel inadequate given her level of experience and awesomeness (it also astounds me that she still has a BlackBerry). But the lesson is clear. Believe in yourself, obey your own boundaries, and push the swing with both hands.

We need to flip the idea that parenthood somehow undermines competence. Senior staff, both men and women, should set an example by taking up extended parental leave, talking about their children in the workplace, and encouraging others to take up flexibility. This sends a positive message to everyone in the organization and makes parenting a superpower in the workplace. Parents are patient negotiators, nurturers of creativity, they are tolerant, they are resilient, they have empathy. They've developed these incredible skills outside of work, which can be transferred into the workplace. Parents are the undiscovered rock stars: in a business world beset with uncertainty, we desperately need people with experience and empathy who can get shit done. As my friend says, "After all, who's more efficient than someone maintaining three projects and a couple of kids every day?"

But the most important sign that flexible working will actually work is if you're working in a high-trust environment. Some pioneering companies are leading the way. One of the ways companies like Netflix and LinkedIn demonstrate their trust in their workers is to offer unlimited paid time off. As long as employees' work is done, and their boss approves, they can take as much paid holiday as they want. Netflix explains: "It's part of our freedom and responsibility culture that we trust employees to balance doing a great job with having a balanced life."

Businesses *can* change their ways and their systems to make flexibility work—and it shouldn't all be down to the employee. However, I've spoken to a range of business leaders, heads of HR, and CEOs and I've listened to their fears around flex. What follows are my tips on how to ask for flexible work and what you can do to make it work once you have it.

"We need to flip the idea that parenthood somehow undermines competence."

HOW TO ASK FOR
FLEX & MAKE IT WORK

1. **Frame your request for flexible working in terms of what it will bring to the business.** This might be the injection of ideas and influences from outside that you will bring back. It might be the contacts you make, the skills you will develop, the emotional energy that you will replenish. Banish the fear that you'll slack off. (And please don't slack off. It breaks the trust and ruins things for the rest of us.)

2. **Show your commitment to the business.** Explain how this longer-term arrangement will work better with your life and needs and therefore will actually make you *more* committed to your job. Banish the fear that flexibility is one foot out of the door.

3. **Remain contactable.** If you want to work remotely a few days a week, explain how contactable you can be and use tools that keep you connected (Google Hangouts for meetings, Google Docs for shared document writing). Slack, a private space for workplace team messaging and sharing, is a great tool to make you feel part of a team even if you are not in the office. It's good for both sharing knowledge and also the little stuff like funny cat gifs.

It's important that flex doesn't isolate you; even though you don't have the same rhythms as the rest of the team, you still need to feel like you belong.

4. **If you are working fewer days or hours, be explicit with your colleagues when you are working and when you are not.** Set up a clear out-of-office email with the times you will answer emails and the times you are out of contact. And then obey your own rules. That bears repeating—obey your own rules! If you set a precedent of replying to emails on your days off, you'll unleash the genie. You need to feel confident in your own abilities and be strong in order to resist any diligent urge you have to get back to people immediately.

SUMMARY

A workforce sitting for long hours every day in the office is not a team of people doing their best work: they are more likely to be stressed and burned out, feeling underappreciated, unable to care in the way they want to for the people they love, and prepared to leave in a second if they could find a job that offers them the flex they crave.

The conversation about flexible working needs to change. There's a parallel to be made with the issue of diversity in the workplace. The language has changed toward "inclusion"—it's not enough to be diverse, although that is a start. We need to be truly inclusive and leave the old boys' club and the "in-jokes" behind. To make a diverse workforce feel genuinely included, we know we need to create the right conditions so they can thrive and do their best work.

Exactly the same shift needs to happen around flexible working. There needs to be a revolution within working culture to acknowledge the failings of rigid and long hours, address "flexism," and actually allow for the *inclusion* of flexible workers. The result will show that flex isn't token, isn't a shitshow, and actually works.

And it needs to work for everyone, not just mothers. We need flexibility to work for older people, for men, for young people entering the workforce, and, of course, for the businesses themselves.

This is why I care about flex so deeply. It is for anyone who has a life and a passion outside of work. Sons and daughters who need to be there for elderly parents. Talented people who believe in portfolio careers. Those that simply want to spend a little more time on something outside the four walls of their job. Flex is for any of us. And any of us should be able to make it work.

FLEX

YOUR

HOME

I'm standing on a stage in a very beige auditorium, about to give a speech to an audience of clients who are all staring at their phones. They seem drugged by the venue's wilting pastries and bad coffee. I'm taking a breath. My heels are too high, my mouth is dry. I have my PowerPoint slides projected on a screen behind me, the clicker in my hand. I'm going to blow their minds with my talk on consumer segmentation. This stuff is gold. Pie charts. Snazzy fonts. I'm totally ready.

But my mind is elsewhere.

Today is my daughter's first day at school. That morning she looked so solemn in her green uniform and shiny shoes, swamped by her giant blazer. She stood on the front doorstep of our home and we took a photo, but her smile was a bit wobbly. The rest of me may be in a conference center, but my heart is with her. I check my watch: it must be morning break right now, she's in the playground. Has she had a snack? Has she got any friends to play with? Is she OK? Is she happy? This dislocated sense of being bodily present at work yet with your heart beating elsewhere is a feeling many of us will recognize.

I remember reading an article by Anne-Marie Slaughter, director of policy planning in the State Department under the Obama administration and the first woman to hold that post. It was titled "Why Women Still Can't Have It All."[23] In it she describes her own tipping point, when she no longer felt she could have it all. "President and Mrs. Obama hosted a glamorous reception. . . . I sipped champagne, greeted foreign dignitaries, and mingled. But I could not stop thinking about my 14-year-old son, who [was] skipping homework, disrupting classes, failing math, and tuning out any adult who tried to reach him."

Slaughter felt it, too, the heart tug. The emotional pivot from work to home. It was a big deal, to me, reading this. An impressive woman saying: This job—a job most of us could only dream of—simply doesn't work for me at this particular moment. Sometimes you can go for it. Sometimes you just can't.

She exposed the cracks when she admitted, "How unexpectedly hard it was to do the kind of job I wanted to do as a high government official and be the kind of parent I wanted to be, at a demanding time for my children."

Slaughter left the job because it didn't allow her to go *with* the grain of life. It required her to put the blinkers on and power through, regardless of what was happening behind the scenes.

This brings me to flex. Home life has its own rhythm, its ebbs and flows. When we embrace flex, we acknowledge those fluctuations. For me, it was my daughter starting school. For Slaughter, it was her teenager going through a tough time. But it could be anything. An elderly parent who has had a fall or a partner's new commute that creates havoc for school drop-offs. It may be that you are moving home, having health problems, or going through a relationship breakup. The tug of home life can be intense at these times; at others it can be imperceptible. Shutting the front door when you leave for work can sometimes feel like an escape. At other times, it feels like abandonment.

It's so easy to see success in terms of career, a job title, a salary raise. But the home is a neglected part of this conversation. Home needs our attention; it needs to feel joyful, it needs to feel happy and balanced. As I will show in this chapter, very often all of this falls on women's shoulders. And it shouldn't. Our partners

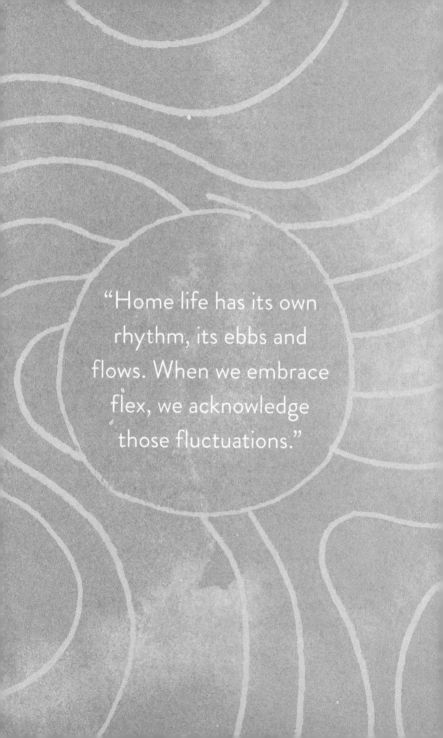

"Home life has its own rhythm, its ebbs and flows. When we embrace flex, we acknowledge those fluctuations."

also need to think about career ambitions, working hours, chores in the home, childcare, and how all of this might flex around the needs of the people in their life.

Here, I will look at how gender relationships in the home are flexing. And I will explain how to spread and share responsibilities in the home and outside of it. This chapter will give you the checklists to be more intentional about your roles. It aims to help you ensure you're not pulled in too many different directions or left carrying the emotional load, which is the invisible—and unrewarded—work of managing the needs of the entire household. And it will give you the conversation starters to have the difficult chats.

WOMEN'S EMOTIONAL LOAD: COPING WITH THE LIST

In the past, roles were clearer. The template was man as breadwinner and woman as homemaker. This still absolutely exists and works for many couples, but it is no longer the norm.

Today, the household comes in all different shapes and sizes. No kids, single parent, two dads or two moms, mom as breadwinner and stay-at-home dad, blended families, dual-income families, beanpole families with more than two generations under one roof—take your pick. The modern family is diverse, impossible to pigeonhole, messy, and beautiful.

And roles within the home are blurring. Over the last half century, in the majority of countries and across all income levels, the number of women working is higher than it was three decades ago.[24]

Most studies report that men are spending more time with their children. Nearly three-quarters of the British public now disagrees with the attitude that women should look after the home while men earn a living. But who does what in the home? That seems to be less clear-cut. With more of us working, with more on everyone's plate, who is keeping the home running?

There are loads of great men out there, doing their share. But the short answer is women. Despite all these societal shifts, so much of work and management of the home still lies with us. Take one of the most mundane and seemingly innocuous parts of life. It's a bellwether for gender equality and a tinderbox to marital relations.

Housework.

The "housework gap" between men and women stopped narrowing back in the late 1990s (until then, women were gradually decreasing the time they spent doing housework as men increased theirs). When it comes to unpaid chores at home, the Office for National Statistics found in 2016 that women do almost 40 percent more than men.[25]

Types of chores are split along gender lines. Women tend to do daily tasks like childcare, laundry, cooking, and cleaning. Men tend to do outdoor chores such as car maintenance and gardening. So, the stuff that needs doing about once a week or less.

So far, so unsurprising. But when we dig into the research, the picture gets a little more complicated.

For a start, same-sex couples are better at chore equality than straight couples. More same-sex, dual-earner couples share laundry and household repair than straight couples. And same-sex couples were much more likely to share childcare equally (74 percent of gay couples versus 38 percent of straight couples). A lesson could be learned from this—neither one is doing the traditional role of

THE IKUMEN PROJECT

In Japan, with its history of salarymen and long working hours, a fascinating cultural change is taking place. The Japanese government, faced with falling birthrates and an aging population, tried to understand why being a mom was less appealing to women. They assumed women felt conflicted about their careers. But they were wrong. Women were avoiding motherhood because they knew their male partners wouldn't do anything to help. But men weren't shirking child-rearing out of sexism or laziness. When surveyed in 2008, a third of working fathers wanted to spend more time with their children and to take paternity leave, but felt their bosses would disapprove.

So the government started the "Ikumen Project" (a melding of Japanese *ikuji,* meaning "child-rearing," and the English "men") with the objective of getting more men involved in bringing up children and making workplaces dad-friendly. In 2009, advertising agency Dentsu invented the term *papa danshi*—"papa men"—to try to make fathers who are "highly motivated in child-rearing" cool. It seemed to work. The percentage of men who took paternity leave increased from 1.9 percent in 2012 to nearly 3 percent in 2015 and 7 percent in 2017. These are not groundbreaking figures, but the seeds of cultural change seem to have been planted.[26]

"mom/wife" or "dad/husband." They are both mucking in and figuring it out, free from gendered expectations of how things "should" be divided.

I love the example of "mommunes," as they are known in America: a group of single mothers and their children sharing one home, supporting each other, creating a new kind of family unit, and dividing up chores between them. One example in the UK is Janet, Vicky, and Nicola's setup in south London. As one of the three moms describes it, "It was like a marriage, only better. We had a kind of invisible rota. We cooked proper dinners for each other every night. We had roles." Janet did the paperwork. Vicky baked. Nicola cooked Sunday dinners and, she says, cleaned up after parties.[27] This is another example of a nontraditional approach that came from experimenting and adapting to each other's strengths.

None of this is easy, mind. A lawyer friend told me about her setup: she is the breadwinner and her partner is at home with the four kids. She stresses the time it took to adapt to these roles. "It was two years of hell adjusting to working while he looked after the kids and house ALL WRONG. We had to gradually let go of gender roles." The people around them needed to let go of them too. "The moms at the school insist on setting up after-school stuff with me. 'Er, I'm in court. I don't know whether the kid can play on Tuesday. Ask his dad.' And others questioned whether their relationship would be affected. People always used to say, 'Oh, don't you/he find the fact he doesn't have a job emasculating?' To which my standard response was, 'No, he's got a massive dick.' True or untrue, it did the job of shutting them up."

It's clearly not as simple as swapping roles.

Women who outearn their partners still do more work in the home. Nearly three-quarters of Americans expect women to have the primary responsibility for cooking at home—even if they spend the same amount of time at work and make more money than their husbands.[28]

And the more they outearn their partners, the less he is willing to do! There is evidence to suggest in households where the woman is the breadwinner, the more she earns, the less he does in the house. It is as though she is being punished for outearning her partner. As the author of one study put it, "We can imagine these men thinking, 'She might earn all the money, but I'm not going to do dishes.' "[29]

I double-take when I read this.
Dishes are really interesting when it
comes to gender roles in the home.

In the research I've read, what's the task that breaks
the camel's back? Washing dishes. Women who say they
wash the majority of dishes report "significantly more
relationship discord, lower relationship satisfaction, and
less sexual satisfaction than women who split the dishes
with their partner."[30] Hold up—less sexual satisfaction?
Men, get the dishwashing liquid out. It's official:
washing dishes can improve your sex life.

It's not just sexual satisfaction that is compromised;
it's women's time too. Women get over 4.5 fewer hours of
leisure time per week than men.[31] That free time is eaten
up by housework as we've seen—but not only that.
A huge amount of list-making, planning, and
choreographing goes on under the surface,
essential to keeping a busy home life
flowing.

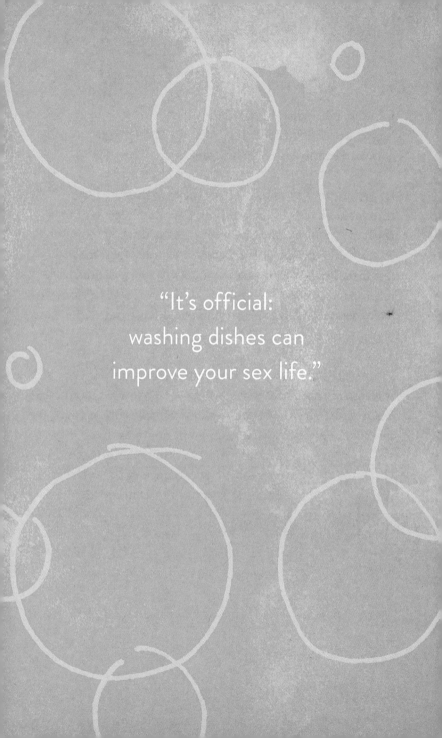

"It's official:
washing dishes can
improve your sex life."

This week, for example, I have a list of tasks hovering on the periphery of my vision:

>> Birthday present for my nephew >> New baby card for my cousin >> Plastic wrap >> Dentist appointments for all of us >> Haircut for daughter no. 1 >> Call friend in Hong Kong >> Check how Mom's mole removal went >> Fix dripping tap >> Give the dog more love >> Packing tape >>

This is known as the emotional load: the unrecognized and unrewarded work that keeps a household running. Managing the emotional load requires great skill. Foresight—knowing that there's a birthday party at the weekend, and the present cupboard is bare. Detail—noticing the children's toenails have become talons and they need declawing. Delegation—can Grandma do the school pickup if we're both working late? Empathy—a friend is going through a divorce, pick up the phone, drop by, be there.

Most of the time, the emotional load is on women's shoulders. One mom told me she doubted her husband even knew which school year her kids were in. Just as we are conditioned to see housework as something suited to women's character, the emotional load is seen as intrinsically female.

It's not. It's just that women are brought up to believe we are better at all of this. Women, we're told, are born nurturers, with natural intuition and empathy.

Society tells us a good woman has her emotional antennae continually quivering, alert to every need of the people surrounding her. In the home, she anticipates, she plans, she remembers, she multitasks—and all of this gives men a pass to be emotionally lazy. None of this is innately female, but it's work that women have absorbed into their lives—so much so that men might be unaware of it going on around them.

The emotional load isn't just made up of booking plumbers and buying birthday cards. During sex, women are still on duty—seemingly giving more attention to their partner's ego than their own pleasure. A study found that 79 percent of women faked an orgasm half of the times they had sex, with the majority believing it boosted their partner's self-esteem (which is why they were doing it in the first place).[32]

Add >> fake orgasm >> boost his mojo >> to that never-ending list . . .

Our leisure time is depleted and, with this constant management of all the emotions that surround us, so is our mental bandwidth. Imagine the ideas and creativity that could burst free if only we weren't thinking about the dog's deworming tablets. Imagine the energy we could give to our families, our friends, our careers, and our health. Imagine our sex lives, if only someone else washed the damn dishes.

We need to look closely at the home and flex these gendered roles, lighten the emotional load, free up our bandwidth, and rechannel our energy. Otherwise we're curbing our own potential.

HOW TO FLEX RELATIONSHIPS & ROLES IN THE HOME

One of the UK's power couples—Justine Roberts, CEO of Mumsnet, and her husband, Ian Katz, director of programming at Channel 4—examined a list of all their responsibilities in the home on a spreadsheet. Both have big jobs and both are equally pressurized outside the home. But when counting their tasks inside the home, Justine had sixty-five and Ian had five (one of his was lightbulbs, and she commented how often they ended up sitting in the dark). She said: "We had a conversation about how we could go about getting a more equal division of labor and he agrees in principle, but it's the practice you have to keep on at."[33]

For a practical solution, look to the Everyday Sexism Project Chore Challenge. They asked couples to keep a two-week log of all the chores (the physical and the emotional) that they do in the home and then gender-swap them.

This might seem extreme. But you could start with just writing down the list for this week and discussing how to share the work. The process of documenting all the work that needs to get done, logging the emotional load, and having the conversation to allocate those jobs is the first step to flexing your roles.

The next priority is to work out who does what. If one person is doing everything and the other person is doing nothing, the relationship will suffer. But tasks don't have to be strictly equal to impact couple satisfaction. It's more important that each individual is clear about their responsibilities, content with their share, and feels like they are making an active choice. Satisfaction is driven more by whether couples talk about how to divide responsibilities than in the precise division of household tasks. We are much more likely to be unsatisfied, or even resentful, if we stay silent instead of voicing our wishes earlier in the relationship.

Clichés of women being better at talking about their issues than men should be banished. A study of 225 couples in the US found that gay men in partnerships were much more likely to say they had discussed how to divide the household labor when they first moved

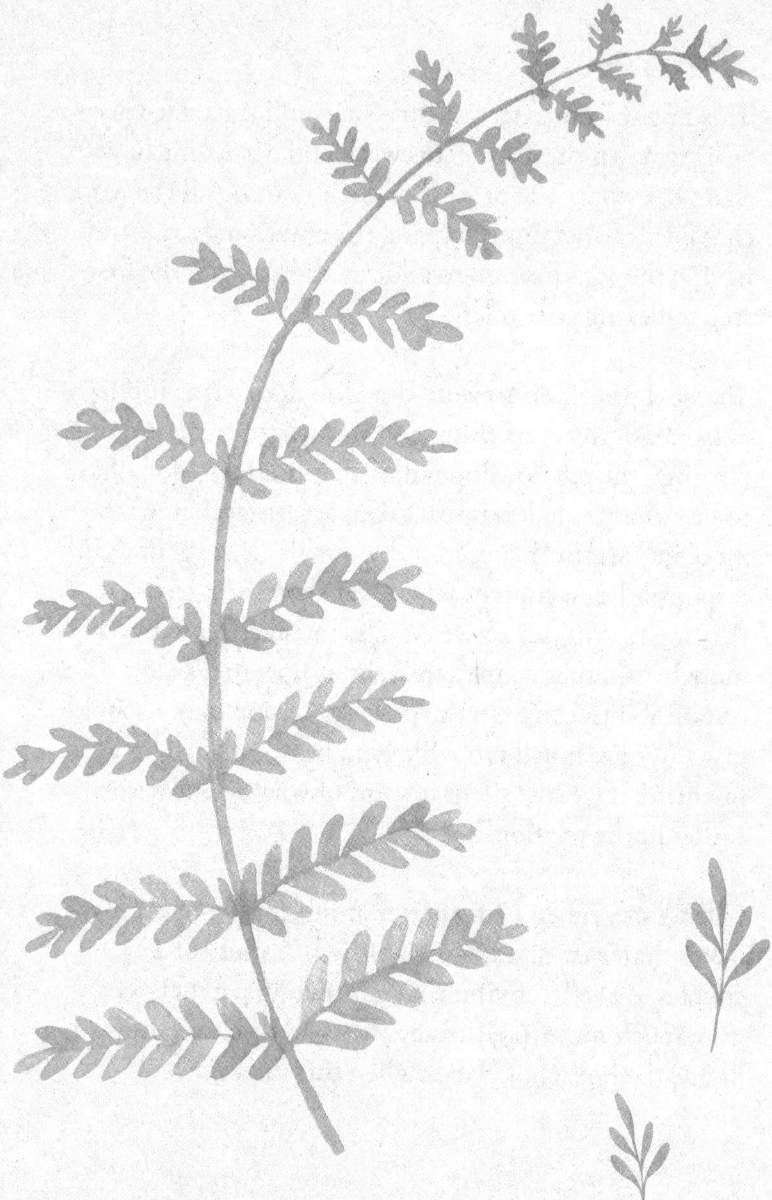

in together. Women in straight partnerships were much more likely to say they wanted to but didn't (and were therefore more unhappy with their domestic arrangements).[34]

So, you've written it down, you've discussed who does what, but don't fall into the trap of having to beg for help every time something needs doing.

The emotional load isn't really lifted if you are compiling lists, micromanaging the tasks, and then asking politely for someone else to do them. It's still on you—you're still the one conducting the boring chore orchestra (the chore-chestra? The bore-chestra?). Perhaps we'll never have true equality until we're all equally bored.

And regarding equality, try to model it for your children. Children scrutinize their parents all the time. They have Sherlock Holmes–like powers of observation. If you have children, be conscious that you are creating templates for them. What are we revealing about our faith in men when we mock "Daddy day care"? What does it say to kids when fathers say they are "babysitting" their own children when Mom goes out? If we want to change gender stereotypes for the next generation, it needs to start with us.

"If we want to
change gender
stereotypes for the
next generation,
it needs to start
with us."

Be aware that men tend to do the outdoor chores that are infrequent and women tend to do everything else. Try to mix it up. Dad, pack for the holidays. Mum, take out the trash bins. Everything might fall apart, but who knows, it might not, and your kids will dislodge their assumptions and expect the load to be shared when they grow up.

CREATE A JOINT VISION

Of course, flexing the home isn't just about the chores. It's about creating a joint vision of the lives we want to live, our career goals, and how that will work over time. We need to think carefully about when we accelerate at work and when we consolidate and slow down. When we do this, we take control.

Avivah Wittenberg-Cox, gender expert and author of *How Women Mean Business*, advocates big-picture thinking. She thinks that it should be less about the jigsaw puzzle of two different careers and more about designing a life together. She asks: "What's the life that we want to build? What are our goals, our mission? What are we going to prioritize, when? Is it family, is it money, is it impact?" Within that framework, where do we flex around each other's ambitions and needs?

One way of thinking about this is the "*Borgen* model." *Borgen* is a Danish political drama television series that aired in the UK in 2012. My friends and I became obsessed with it, in particular the Birgitte Nyborg character, who became the first female prime minister of Denmark. In the series, she had an agreement with her husband, Philip, an academic, that she would have the "lead career" for five years as prime minister, while his career took a back seat and he managed the emotional load, looking after the kids and the home. After this, she would step back and give him his turn. Despite it not quite going as planned, I loved this arrangement and found it inspiring. The generosity of making trade-offs for one another and seeing a bigger picture of joint and intertwined success seemed like a revelation. It is also a bold and proactive approach, rather than just firefighting in response to opportunities or problems.

Now, this need not be a five-year set-in-stone contract. It could be a looser agreement to flex around each other's ambitions.

SHARERS VS. WINNERS

Not everyone is willing to give the *Borgen* model a go. A study of forty-two heterosexual men in mostly dual-earner couples who worked at a global strategy consulting firm exposed stark differences in the men's willingness to flex around their partners' careers. The study divided them into two groups:

~ the "breadsharers": men who believed their wives should equally pursue their work and family goals.

~ the "breadwinners": men who attached low social status to their wives' professions.

The breadsharers were more likely to be open to flexing their own careers and changing jobs, cities, or countries if that might be needed in the future for their wives' careers. A typical quote was: "I want to make sure she continues to be in a professional situation where she can [succeed], and that . . . puts pressure back on me to . . . say, 'OK, wait. Our life is not going to be the one where I get to do whatever I want job-wise, just because my life is not the center.'"

The breadwinners intended to stay at the firm and try their hardest to make partner, and were not willing to flex around their wives' careers. A breadwinner quote: "She could have done much more than she has [in her field], but she chose a different path. What I call, you know—being a project manager in the home . . ." Bear in mind, in this instance, his wife's salary made up one-third of the family's income! You can only flex your home if you have a partner who is open to it. [35]

HELEN DWYER'S FLEX STORY

⊰≫≫ ≪≪⊱

*Helen Dwyer, sixty-three, is a retired school
principal in Bathurst, Australia*

I left school at the age of seventeen. I took up any retail work I could get, met my husband-to-be, and generally had a good time and "fun in the sun" life. I was married at twenty and by the time I was thirty-two I had two children (two and six years old), was virtually working full-time in between a news agency, bakery, and handbag store while my husband worked full-time shift work.

At this stage, my husband and I had a conversation and both decided that I should apply to the university to study for a teaching diploma. We felt this would be a good move to allow us a better lifestyle and a more secure future for our family. It meant we juggled the care of our children, had a mortgage, and lived from week to week. Over the three years it took to gain my qualifications, my husband continued to work shift work and I continued to work part-time. Between us we cared for our children.

We had no family support where we lived, so it really was up to us to work as a team. The childcare was a constant juggle. My eldest, Luke, had started school and my youngest, Gareth, was two when I started at the university. I was able to secure one day per week at the university day care for Gareth, which was not flexible. I would keep my fingers crossed each semester and try to get as much university or library time in on that day. I had a great neighbor who would care for Gareth and Luke after school in the uncovered time gaps. Work was important for both of us due to the cost of the care for Gareth, university costs, and the cost of living.

None of this ever went smoothly! Often we were problem-solving on the run—things like illness (kids, caregivers, or us), timetabling changes at the university, extra shifts at work, and unexpected things that pop up in life. Also, I had six practical assessments in schools over the three years, which would throw everything out of whack. My mother-in-law—God bless her— would leave her home to stay with us for these times.

It paid off as I graduated from the university with distinction, as one of the top ten graduates in my year, and was rewarded with a full-time teaching position with the New South Wales Department of Education.

Fortunately, all of this was a shared goal with my husband. If it weren't, I would never have achieved it. We then were able to live a more comfortable and secure life with our children, and my husband was able to pursue goals of his own. Our children were able to follow their interests with our support. I recently retired as a school principal after a wonderful and fulfilling career in education spanning twenty-seven years.

And that brings us on to the final point. A friend who leads a big institution in the public sector says his staff (often women) are increasingly coming to him with requests for more flexible working. He is pleased that these conversations are happening, but he questions whether, in some instances, flexible working will solve the deeper problems at play.

"People come to me and talk about flex, and I want to say, 'Go and talk to your husband.' The conversation should start at home." In some of these instances, the woman is bending her career and her life around an intractable male partner's job, or his refusal to take on any of the domestic load. She is flexing, but is progress really being made?

We should flex, but we shouldn't become contortionists, bending over backward. And we all need to start the conversation at home.

HOW TO FLEX
YOUR HOME

1. Write down all the chores that are done in the home. In Excel if you're fancy, on the back of an unopened bill if you're not. Be awe-inspired at the amount you are currently doing. Be shocked at how little anyone else is doing.

2. Allocate some time with your partner to discuss who does what. You could start by working through each room of the house and noting jobs associated with that room. You could then think in terms of tasks that are daily (cooking, cleaning, childcare), weekly (food shopping, scheduling playdates), and yearly (purchasing insurance, the car's inspection). It's not about a 50/50 split. It's about being happy with your lot.

3. Be sensitive. This conversation may be fraught, especially if either party feels resentful at the amount they are currently doing. A good way to approach things would be to appreciate and acknowledge what each of you is doing before explaining what you would like help with. Then negotiate. You may hate doing the laundry but not mind doing the vacuuming. Could you use that as a bargaining tool?

4. Model good behaviors for your children so they don't just associate women with home and men with work. Men: mop floors. Women: mow the lawn.

5. Don't micromanage the to-do list, or feel like you need to beg for help each time something needs doing. Don't end up being the "conductor of the chore-chestra." Encourage your partner to proactively take responsibility for a whole task area. For example, whoever is in charge of school shoes needs to know the children's shoe sizes and when they've grown out of them, and arrange to buy new ones.

6. Discuss a longer-term vision of the lives you want to live and work out priorities within that. How can you and your partner flex around each other? Think about the *Borgen* model. Might it work for you? What other model could work?

SUMMARY

Flex is more than a Band-Aid solution to see you through changing times at home. Permission to flex between home and work is liberating. Permission to define success in the way we want to—whether it is raising a family or raising hell at work—is liberating.

We need to turn our attention to what is happening inside our homes, relationships, and families. The modern household looks and feels different from the one we grew up in. Roles within it are less clearly defined, and day-to-day life feels more complex. We add more and more items to our mental lists. We're negotiating gender roles, both in the home and outside, which means that everything is up for grabs.

We need to be OK with that and take inspiration from pioneering nontraditional units, like mommunes, gay couples, and stay-at-home dads. By creating new models and forging new paths, they are paving the way for the households of the future. Like them, we need to experiment, to invent, to work out what kind of life we really want to live with the people who are most precious to us. We should think about how best to achieve that, together. We need to talk it through, because things are changing under our noses. Work is important, but home matters the most, and just because our roles and relationships are bending, they don't need to break.

FLEX

& THE

BODY

When I talk about flex and the body, I'm not referring to exercise and stretching (although I highly approve of both). This chapter is less about the ability to touch your toes and more about the skill of really listening to your body and flexing your life to work *with* it rather than *against* it.

It's only recently that I started listening to my body. For most of my adult life, I treated it as a sort of machine to propel me through life. Sometimes the machine fired on all cylinders, but at other times it ground to a halt and I grew impatient. I drank an extra coffee if I felt tired, I dosed up with OTC remedies if a cold was brewing, I took a painkiller when I had menstrual cramps.

Forcing myself to carry on as normal, while practical and sometimes necessary in the short term, doesn't work for me anymore. It ignores my body's rhythms, moods, and cycles. It meant I ended up doing things like writing a detailed report when my brain was distracted (resulting in tea breaks, Twitter binges, muddled thinking, and little work). Or throwing a party when I'm at my most insecure (take it from me—hermit-like host plus awkward guests is not a recipe for fun times). So I started to realize that ignoring my body is not very smart.

"Sometimes, it ain't exactly broke, but it does need fixing."

Much of my body-as-machine attitude is inherited. My parents have a rigid approach to health. You are either at death's door or you need to pull your socks up and get on with it. For them, doctors are quacks and catastrophe-mongers and should be avoided at all costs. On health, their mantra is "If it ain't broke, don't fix it."

But sometimes, it ain't exactly broke, but it does need fixing. When I was thirty-seven, I felt exhausted most of the time. I had two little girls under the age of six. I didn't really exercise, unless you counted the speed walking I did around London every day to get to the train station, to the office, to the nursery. I slept terribly, falling into an exhausted slumber by 10 p.m. every night only to awaken at 3 a.m. with creeping dread. My washing-machine brain churned over fragments of my day, which were perfectly ordinary but in the lonely predawn seemed filled with menace. I realized something had to change, and for me that was sleep.

Sleep is such a mysterious part of life. Every one of us, on average, will sleep twenty-four years in our lifetime. That's twenty-four years of dreams we forget. Twenty-four years of repair and restoration that we take for granted. Twenty-four years of inhaled flies and drool-soaked pillows. If we have a lifelong partner, that's likely to be a good ten years of shared slumber, unconscious battles over covers, tender, intertwined limbs, and fogs of morning breath. We take no notice of this huge chunk of our lives, until it evades us.

My insomnia was a message from my body I couldn't ignore. I made a decision then, aged thirty-seven, that I was going to address my sleep issues. It started me on a different journey, that of understanding my body more holistically.

In this chapter, I examine two areas of women's lives that often get neglected—sleep and periods. The better we understand them, and our rhythms and moods, the better we are able to flex our schedules and our expectations so that we can perform at our best and happiest.

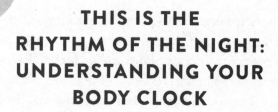

THIS IS THE RHYTHM OF THE NIGHT: UNDERSTANDING YOUR BODY CLOCK

Our body clocks are governed by circadian rhythms—physical, mental, and behavioral patterns that follow a twenty-four-hour cycle: *circum* means "around," *dies* means "day."

The average rhythm during a day is that we warm up and reach peak alertness at around noon. This peak then decreases until about 3 p.m.—the slump when we usually reach for a cup of coffee, a snack, or a can of cola. In some parts of the world, like Spain, this is the time when people take a siesta. After this trough, our alertness tends to climb toward a second high at around 6 p.m. Then it's a steady decline to 3:30 a.m. After this, alertness climbs again and the cycle repeats the following day.

Bizarre, then, that peak alertness for the average person comes at noon, just when we're about to head off to lunch, and at 6 p.m., when we're probably commuting home. In terms of the standard workday, at least, this can represent a huge lost opportunity.

However, individuals do vary in their patterns of alertness. Some of us have a genetic predisposition to function really well in the morning ("larks") or perform better in the evening ("owls"). Those who fall somewhere in between, and relate to the average rhythm, are "hummingbirds." This is your chronotype: your body's natural timeline for eating, sleeping, and working.

I'm probably the love child of a hummingbird and an owl (a howl?). If my children didn't wake me up every day at 6:30 a.m., I'd happily sleep until 9 a.m. As it stands, I'm groggy and slow in the mornings. Whenever I'm on the subway in the morning rush hour, jammed into someone's armpit, I take refuge in headphones and coffee. Between the hours of 10 a.m. and noon I'm on fire. This is when I feel efficient, creative, and get shit done. This stops at 12:30 p.m., when I'm suddenly ravenous. After lunch, I chug along nicely until about 4 p.m., when I slip into first gear. If I'm at work, I need a cup of tea and a chat about my latest podcast obsession. If I'm at home, I need to stand in front of the fridge eating handfuls of cheese. Post-cheese, there's another mini-peak (a fun conversation over dinner, or I might dive into some efficient work) before bed at 11 p.m.

Whether you are a lark, an owl, or a hummingbird is driven by differing levels of the two hormones involved in regulating sleep. Cortisol rises in the morning and powers us to wake up. Melatonin increases in the evening and helps wind our bodies down for sleep. For night owls, melatonin rises later in the day than the average, while cortisol increases earlier than average for morning larks.

And this doesn't remain stable—our body clocks change throughout our lives. As a child enters teenage years, pubertal hormones shift the body clock by one to two hours, which means teens become owl-ish, and naturally sleep and wake later during adolescence. Blamed for being lazy, teens are actually just adapting to a new rhythm of their body clock. Teens need about eight to ten hours of sleep each night to function best. And because they are falling asleep later, but still have to get up at the same time for school, most teens are sleep-deprived—one study found that only 15 percent reported sleeping eight and a half hours on school nights.[36]

How many of us remember those teenage mornings of feeling exhausted and grumpy? How many of us are now coping with teens who need to be pried out of bed? Life today, with its dominant rhythm of 9 a.m.–5 p.m.

for workers and 8:30 a.m.–4 p.m. for students, is better suited to larks. Owls build up a sleep debt over time, which results in health issues; owls have higher rates of depression and anxiety.

For night-shift workers, this is amplified. As well as the health fallout from irregular eating habits and interrupted sleep, they can also feel out of sync with their loved ones, which may chip away at their well-being.

An owl friend who is also a shift worker talks of her dislocation from her friends. When she meets them for a meal, she isn't hungry at the right time. When she wants to chat, they are going to bed. I often wake up to a bunch of WhatsApp messages she sends me overnight—we are in different emotional time zones, desperate to get onto the same page.

We should do as much as possible to flex our activities to fit with the natural circadian rhythms of the day, and our chronotype within that. The timetables of those doing night-shift work will be very different, and flexing work hours may not be possible in all industries. But what follows are some thoughts on how you might be able to flex your days and weeks to work with your natural body clock.

ARE YOU A LARK, AN OWL, OR A HUMMINGBIRD?

~ Decide your chronotype—in other words, whether you are a lark, an owl, or a bit of both. Around 10 percent of us are larks and 20 percent are owls—the rest of us, known as hummingbirds, fall somewhere in between.

~ Larks tend to sleep between the hours of 10 p.m. and 6 a.m., or earlier. Larks find it hard to sleep in, even if they have gone to bed later. Peak productivity is around noon, and they fizzle out in the early evening.

~ Owls tend to stay awake until past midnight, and would wake after 10 a.m. if they could. Peak productivity is the middle of the day and the evening.

~ Hummingbirds wake up at 7 a.m. and go to bed around 11 p.m. They tend to be alert throughout the average nine-to-five day but slump in the early afternoon.

TIPS FOR LARKS

~ Larks can fit in morning exercise before the day gets started.

~ Larks are great at doing the school run calmly, getting everyone out the door and on time to school, whereas other chronotypes might find it pressurized and fraught.

~ Larks should do their most challenging work first thing. Avoid distractions in the late morning around your noon peak. Can you switch off emails until the afternoon, which will allow you to focus, undistracted?

~ Think about a mid-morning snack to keep you going at 10 a.m.

~ Larks should do their more routine work—answering emails and nondemanding admin, for example—in the afternoon.

~ Arrange social activities over lunch and coffees in the week, so you're not pushing yourself to be fun when you'd rather be curled up in bed with a book.

~ Larks should begin winding down at 9:30 p.m. and turn off all screens. The blue light from devices activates your brain and makes it harder to go to sleep.

~ If possible, can you flex your working day to start at 7 a.m. and finish at 3 p.m.?

TIPS FOR OWLS

~ Owls will be rushed in the morning. Can you pack school bags or set out clothes for the next day the night before?

~ Could you also make your breakfast the previous evening? That way you won't miss breakfast or have to flap about when you are half asleep.

~ If at work, use the morning for routine work and planning—answer emails, create lists, plan ahead.

~ Try not to schedule meetings or socialize before lunch, when you might still be in first gear.

~ Owls should do their difficult, most brain-taxing work after lunch.

~ Owls should think about flexing around the second peak at about 6 p.m. If you can leave later and miss commuter rush hour, you could achieve great things in a focused period in the early evening. The benefit is that everyone else will have gone home, so the email flow should slow down, giving you undistracted time.

~ Find a time to work out after 6 p.m., when you're most energetic.

~ If possible, can you flex your working day to start at 11 a.m. and finish at 7 p.m.?

TIPS FOR HUMMINGBIRDS

~ The nine-to-five is best suited to the hummingbird.
~ Peak productivity is at noon—a good time for 30 minutes of concentrated work, a workout, or blitzing some housework.
~ Have a snack at about 3 p.m., when you might need a pick-me-up.
~ If you have problems sleeping, avoid foods rich in fat or sugar late at night as these will be difficult to digest.
~ If you tend to putter around in the late evening and find it hard to wind down, consider setting an alarm to remind you to go to bed.

Sleep is the magic formula for a better life. The first thing we need to do is value it and make sure we get enough of it. Scientists have shown that a good night's sleep leads to happier, more creative, longer lives. But we can go further than that. Tweaking your daily activities to fit your chronotype means you can personalize your routine and live and work at your best. When I began to understand my sleep rhythms, it was a revelation. The next rhythm I wanted to understand was my menstrual cycle.

ABOUT BLOODY TIME: UNDERSTANDING PERIODS

My generation was taught to associate periods with shame. We were not to talk about them, we were to hide tampons up our sleeves on our way to the toilet and to see bleeding as messy and inconvenient. It was a female zone, not fit for male attention or conversation.

Even the language we used showed shame. Go to a drugstore and you'd see shelves of "feminine hygiene" or "sanitary products"—arguably male language to describe a natural process that is neither unhygienic nor unsanitary.

Menstrual advertising coyly showed blue liquid, as though blood was too disgusting to acknowledge. The message from these ads was loud and clear. They said: "We get you. We get those damn inconvenient, unpleasant, embarrassing periods. Don't worry, we've got your back (and by 'your back,' we mean your pad). We'll get you back to normal again (and by 'normal,' we mean Rollerblading™ and kitesurfing)."

But I didn't want to get back to normal. I WAS normal. It *is* normal to bleed every month, so why were we in a state of frenzied, shameful denial?

Before we can flex around our periods, the first thing we have to do is talk about them. And this is starting to happen. A de-shaming revolution is happening, and periods have risen on the cultural agenda. Period poverty is a campaigning hotspot, with people like 21-year-old north London schoolgirl and founder of #FreePeriods Amika George campaigning for girls who qualify for free school meals to also get free menstrual products.

More recent menstrual product advertising has started to tackle some bold topics. Bodyform was the first brand to show blood in advertisements instead of the industry standard of blue liquid in their "Blood Normal" campaign.

Businesses and governments have begun to respond too. Nike has had menstrual leave in their code of conduct since 2007. In some countries, governmental legislation offering menstrual leave exists already, yet take-up is low, as women fear they will be judged and their chances of promotion will fall. But what is the point of legislation if women don't benefit from it? Periods are still a source of shame.

Talking about them at work is still seen as detrimental to your professionalism. Who among us would approach a male boss, tampon in hand, and say: "I'm cramping with period pain and bleeding like a bastard, so I'm going home to down some ibuprofen and watch Netflix in bed."

Dr. Jan Toledano, a specialist at the London Hormone Clinic, agrees. "Society is not very forgiving, and women

MENSTRUAL LEAVE AROUND THE WORLD

Menstrual leave has been a legal right for Japanese women since 1947, granting women with period pain *seirikyuuka* or "psychological leave." South Korea introduced a law in 2001 that allows women to take one day of menstrual leave per month. In 2016, the Chinese province of Anhui became the third Chinese province to introduce period leave, allowing women with severe menstrual pain to take one to two days off every month, on presenting a doctor's certificate.

are expected to fit in with the workplace. There is massive pressure for women to carry on as usual despite their symptoms."

The fact remains that before we can begin to flex around our cycles, we need to change the conversation around periods and break the taboos.

All around us, the conversation about periods is changing. It's a crucial topic for flex. Throughout our cycles, hormone levels fluctuate making us feel, behave, and perform differently as we move through the month. The changes in levels of progesterone and estrogen affect brain cognition, emotions, sensory processing, and appetite (as well as the performance-related aspects Emma Hayes mentions on page 134). It makes sense to lean into these changes rather than fear them. If we adjust our routines, social lives, and work behaviors to suit our bodies, it stands to reason we could feel, live, and work better.

This is called cycle syncing. Understanding your cycle and adjusting life to suit it is a form of self-care, of being kind to yourself. Can you put yourself forward for the activities and social engagements that will make you feel happy and fulfilled rather than inhibited and like you're failing?

TABOO-BREAKING IN SPORTS

The conversation around periods is changing in the traditionally macho world of sports. Serena Williams was at the frontier back in 2005 when she talked about her menstrual migraines. In 2015, British tennis player Heather Watson talked—euphemistically, but at least she spoke up—of "girl things" when she was beaten in the Australian Open, and Kiran Gandhi, drummer for British–Sri Lankan rapper M.I.A., ran the London Marathon while on her period "free-bleeding," using no menstrual product, with blood running down her legs.

In women's soccer in the UK, Emma Hayes was the coach of Chelsea Ladies when they won the League and FA Cup double in 2018. She has studied the impact of menstrual cycles on players' reaction times, manual dexterity, neuromuscular coordination, blood sugar levels, and muscle maintenance.

"This subject is pushed away like a taboo, but it's important," Hayes says. "If I had unlimited resources, I would hire someone to manage my players' menstrual cycles."[37] Imagine the "marginal gains" that could be made by analyzing the team's cycles and changing game plans accordingly. If male athletes had periods, there would be teams of people researching and monitoring them. Understanding the physiological and emotional impact of cycles could be a game-changer outside of sports too. If we can flex our personal game plans to sync with our cycles, it could help us achieve our own peak performance.

GO WITH YOUR FLOW

"Everyone has a different cycle," says Toledano. "Some don't have any symptoms at all, but some are quite incapacitated, which can last half the month. This can impact cognitive function, which affects work. We can feel clumsy, foggy—we can't think straight."

I relate to this. My mental and emotional state changes throughout my cycle. At some points, I feel confident, extroverted, and my mood is buoyant. But nearing my period, I can feel anxious, inhibited, and tend to catastrophize. An unanswered WhatsApp translates to "my friend hates me." My daughter's tummy ache sends me scrambling to Dr. Google for terrifying possible diagnoses. It took until my late thirties to spot the patterns in these feelings and see them as cyclical rather than permanent personality traits. I used a period-tracking app to document my symptoms and feelings, and gradually I became able to anticipate moods and actually flex my life around my cycle. And I'm not alone. The rise of period-tracking apps like Clue and Flow are a testament to an appetite to understand our bodies and cycles better.

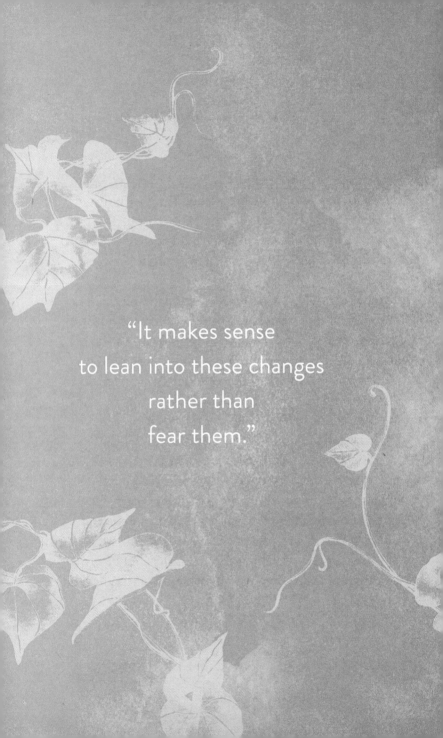

"It makes sense
to lean into these changes
rather than
fear them."

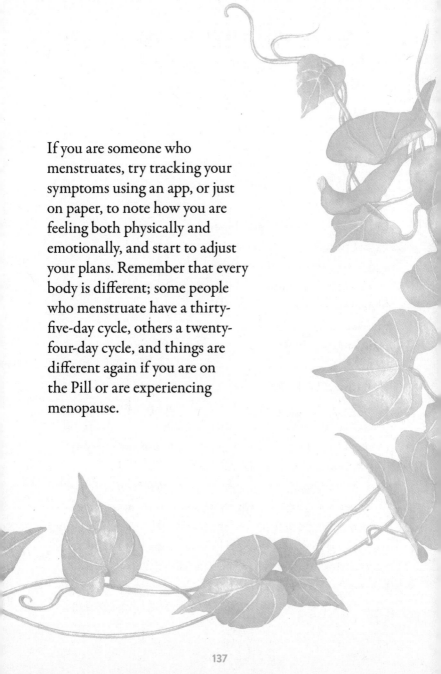

If you are someone who menstruates, try tracking your symptoms using an app, or just on paper, to note how you are feeling both physically and emotionally, and start to adjust your plans. Remember that every body is different; some people who menstruate have a thirty-five-day cycle, others a twenty-four-day cycle, and things are different again if you are on the Pill or are experiencing menopause.

KATE SHEPHERD COHEN'S
FLEX STORY

*Kate Shepherd Cohen is a menstrual coach
and educator*

My period was never "my" time of the month at all. It belonged to everyone else, just like every other day: friends and family and their needs; community and consumerism and their needs. It was a continuous sensation of being and feeling stuck in an outward-looking, ego-driven, high-energy motivational state: meetings every minute, late nights every night, and alarms going off too early every morning. I began to suffer. Every two weeks, I felt deeply depressed and almost suicidal. It took me a long time to work out it was cyclical. I was diagnosed with PMDD [premenstrual dysphoric disorder]—severe PMS, which the doctor said was treatable through the contraceptive pill and antidepressants. My cycle was seen as an illness and a disorder.

I realized how little I knew about the menstrual cycle. I thought back to my biology lessons at school and vaguely remembered the diagram of the uterus and its thickening lining being shed. That's where my knowledge ended. How could this be, after twenty-five years of menstruation? Three hundred five-day periods! That's roughly 1,500 days of my life thought of, at best, as an inconvenience. My menstrual mission began in that moment. I swore to live by the natural rhythms of my own cycle, to harness the changing energies of my menstrual cycle. I soon discovered the work of menstrual godmothers Lucy H. Pearce, Alexandra Pope and Sjanie Hugo Wurlitzer (founders of the Red School), and Miranda Gray, among others.

From not knowing where I was in my cycle and it wreaking havoc, it's now a central part of my life and supports me in everything we do as a family, to the point of proudly having my menstrual clock (with the hand pointing to the day of my cycle) hanging in our kitchen.

This clock is divided into quarters, showing the four seasons of my cycle, and lets the whole family know where I am. My husband loves it—he sees it as a road map to understanding me. He can see where I am—for example, if I was overly critical, he wouldn't take that personally. The clock gives me boundaries. In autumn I don't take on any new projects. I think about winter approaching, and I start to say no to socializing. It is significant to have the clock in the kitchen, in a public place, not in a shameful, hidden one. Women are at the heart of families; if our natural cycles are respected, everyone benefits.

The positive ripple effect of this cyclical self-care is enormous. It makes perfect sense that following deep rest for three days, I'm recharged and ready for the remainder of the month, able to be the best person I can be and of greater service to others. Living in harmony with the menstrual cycle (and being supported to do so), I believe, is the key to true feminine liberation.

HOW TO FLEX
WITH YOUR CYCLE

One way to understand your menstrual cycle is to think of the four phases as seasons, as Kate Shepherd Cohen does, and try to flex your activities around those seasons.

1. **Winter: Menstrual phase (days 1 to 7)**

BODY: Your estrogen and progesterone levels are low; your uterus sheds its lining. You have your period. At this time, you bleed and you might experience backache, tiredness, and food cravings. Testosterone production boosts sex drive during the period.

MIND: You might feel tired, withdrawn, and antisocial. Rather than forcing yourself to plod on as usual, this is your cue to look after yourself and conserve energy. See this time as a treat and a retreat from the crazed pace of everyday life. An overloaded schedule is likely to push you over the edge. Learn to say no, elegantly. Enjoy going for walks, reading, and making delicious meals. You might binge-watch a TV series or have lots of sex, riding the wave of high libido. Might be hard to do both, depending on how good the series is.

2. **Spring: Follicular phase (days 8 to 13)**

BODY: In this phase, your body is preparing to ovulate (release an egg). Your estrogen levels start to increase from their decline in the menstrual phase, and your uterus lining builds up with blood, tissue, and nutrients to prepare for implantation of the fertilized egg.

MIND: As estrogen levels rise, you may be buzzing, physically energized, mentally alert, and positive about the future. It's a fresh start. At work, you're on fire. You are smart and productive. You say clever things and resist the urge to mic drop when you leave a room. You learn quicker, so it's a great time for creativity and gaining new skills. See this time as a procrastination killer, start something you've been putting off. "Spring" is for risk-taking and pushing your boundaries—you're in the zone.

3. Summer: Ovulatory phase (days 14 to 21)

BODY: Ovulation begins. The egg is released on its journey down the fallopian tube. If it meets sperm on this journey, it will become fertilized. Estrogen levels are peaking and testosterone also rises. You may feel pelvic pain or twinges—this has a lovely name for something so unlovely: *Mittelschmerz*, which means "middle pain" in German. You may experience bloating and painful boobs.

MIND: High estrogen makes you bolder, more confident, and ready for a challenge. Social skills are at their highest—you are super-fun. New friends think you're the bee's knees, old friends remember why they liked you in the first place. Testosterone also rises, which means you can feel more impulsive, daring, and competitive. And when testosterone spikes, it boosts your libido. See this as a phase for socializing, sex, and superpowers.

4. **Autumn: Luteal phase (days 22 to 28)**

BODY: Estrogen levels drop off during this phase and progesterone increases. You could experience PMS symptoms like acne, sleep disturbances, mood changes, and cramping.

MIND: Progesterone is a sedating, antianxiety hormone. You might feel brooding and cautious. You might have bouts of sadness or crying. You might want to be surrounded by close friends who love and understand you, or you may want to hide from the world. Your brain is primed for detail rather than big-picture thinking. See "Autumn" as a time to slow down, get your life in order, and plan. Winter is coming, friends. Winter is coming.

SUMMARY

We should delight in the body rather than fear it, listen to it rather than ignore it. We should talk about our cycles and mood fluctuations rather than feel ashamed of them. Pioneers in the world of sports, sleep, and wellness are treating the female body as an undiscovered country, exploring it and understanding its idiosyncrasies. We can use that knowledge to flex our behaviors to perform, work, and live better.

I used to periodically feel tired, overwhelmed by life, and as if I was failing. Now, I try to flex my day to work with my "hummingbird"/"owl" chronotype. I am more conscious of my menstrual cycle and try to schedule big events to avoid my "Autumn" and coincide with my "Summer." It doesn't work all the time, as sometimes it's impossible to flex my calendar. But by trying, I feel more in control and no longer on the back foot. It has been a revelation. I'm kinder to myself, I respect my moods and my boundaries, and, for me, it's a more sustainable way to live.

FLEX

~

YOUR

~

FUTURE

When I was little, all adults asked children the same question: "What do you want to be when you grow up?" Kids were trained to answer this. We picked something and stuck to it. I wanted to be a vet. My best friend Katie wanted to be an astronaut. Another kid—and this begs its own set of questions—wanted to be Pretty Woman. The idea was, as children, we were not yet our true selves. At some point we'd be "grown-up" and, at that moment, our identity would crystallize. The floaty bits of us would snap into focus and we'd solidify into the person we were meant to be. And we'd stay that same self. Our careers would be our identities. I would be a vet. Vet-ness would run through me like a stick of hard candy.

I'm not a vet. The closest I ever came to being one was having a dog. The question was flawed from the start. Adults still ask it, but I've noticed that children tend to answer "I don't know" these days. My daughter tells me she thinks it's a stupid question. "It changes all the time, Mommy. How can we know?"

She's right—how can we know? Independent forecaster the Institute for the Future predicted that almost half of today's jobs may be replaced by automation in the next twenty years.[38] Some jobs, like accountants, cashiers, call center operators, bank tellers, and pharmacists, may

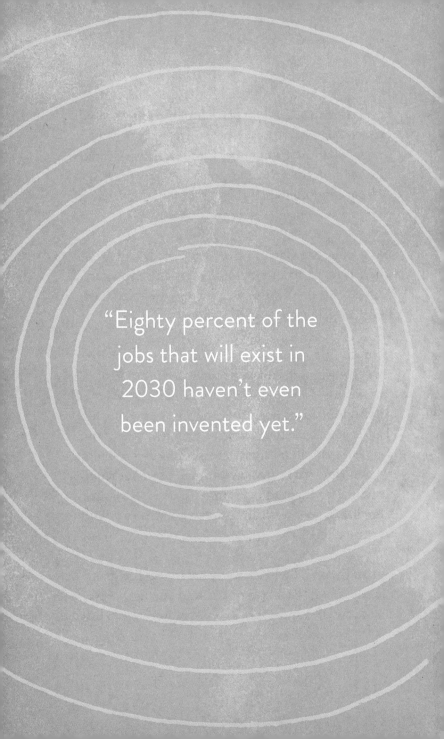

"Eighty percent of the jobs that will exist in 2030 haven't even been invented yet."

become extinct. And 80 percent of the jobs that will exist in 2030 haven't even been invented yet. Who knows what these might be? Drone traffic controllers? End-of-life coaches? Telesurgeons? Techno-ethicists? Asking children to nail their ambitions down to a job that may no longer exist is nonsensical.

None of us can plan our lives forensically and rationally. There is no perfect route forward, with all the stars aligned. We don't know what's coming—maybe we never have, but now we really don't.

Globally, life spans are increasing, our working lives are getting longer, and we're facing a multitude of transitions—in love, in jobs, in life—along the way. This uncertainty opens up a whole new way of seeing life. This is not a time for definitive, rigid ten-year plans. It's a time for continual education, skilling and reskilling, side-hustling, and career pivots—all of which require flexibility to adapt to new circumstances. It's a time, as Oprah said, to "step into the new story you are willing to create."

In this chapter, I will look at what longer life spans, new life paths, and the march of artificial intelligence mean for the way we live and work. I'll look at how we can listen to our intuition and make decisions that pivot us in new directions. And I'll explore why flex is so important to future-proof ourselves, and live happy, fulfilled, long lives.

PLOT TWIST!
LETTING GO OF LIFE STAGES

No one knows the amount of time each of us has left on this earth. What is undeniable is that we are living longer. In the 1840s, British people lived, on average, until they were forty. That's roughly my age as I write this. Today, more than one in four children born in the UK can expect to reach 100. In France, it is one in two.

With these longer lives stretching out ahead of us, blocks of time associated with distinct life stages are swapping and muddling together. Older people are going back to school and retraining. Younger people are leapfrogging higher education and becoming entrepreneurs. Marriage and children are delayed, or outright rejected. People of different ages and levels of experience will be studying, working, socializing together.

What is clear is that life is no longer a three-act play with a distinct beginning, middle, and end. It doesn't start with education, continue with work, and end with retirement. Rather, it's a collage of time hops and plot twists, a mishmash of experimentation and adaptation. So we need to let go of rigid assumptions of what young adulthood, midlife, and older age are about.

Careers, today, are not for life. Today's learners will have eight to ten jobs by the time they are thirty-eight. This trend has been termed the "quitting economy," and it involves switching between jobs as a way to get higher wages, accumulate experience and contacts, and avoid the stagnation of a fixed path. Quitting is no longer "for losers"; it is a shrewd way to get ahead, to continually reinvent and resell yourself.

THE RISE OF THE SIDE HUSTLE

According to a recent report called *The Side Hustle Economy*, as many as one in four adults are side-hustling, and these hustles generate income worth £72 billion for the UK. Emma Gannon, author of *The Multi-Hyphen Method*, says it is working for her: "The ability to have more flexible working, to work on my own side projects, add different themes and strands to my work and personal identity . . . have all added to my own personal definition of success."[39]

This capacity for reinvention is also expressed in the rise of side projects. These have been termed "side hustles" and are usually defined as a small business or supplementary job on top of a main career to boost income, fulfill a passion, or both.

Some worry about this more flexible approach to working and blame it on a generational lack of loyalty. They say young people are always looking for something new, always obsessed with whether they feel "fulfilled." But to view it like this is to misunderstand the game. It's not just out of choice. They are quitting and switching jobs and side-hustling because they have to.

Today's young people are at risk of being the first generation since the Second World War to earn less than their parents. It is the precariousness of this changing world that forces young people to adapt and shape-shift in order to keep on the front foot. Without the safety net and economic buoyancy of their parents' generation, they have to flex. And these skills will become more and more crucial for them as they age and the job market continually changes shape.

As people approach their forties, the markers of adulthood their parents bought into are becoming fainter and fainter. People aren't following the traditional grown-up script as much anymore—buying property, getting married, having children. They complain about

THE DECLINE OF "ADULT" MILESTONES

The ultimate symbol of settling down, homeownership, is out of reach for the majority today. It is declining globally as house prices are rising in every major city and incomes are not keeping up. A 2017 report published by estate agents Knight Frank predicted that almost one in four households in Britain will be renting privately by the end of 2021 because of unaffordable house prices and stagnant wages.[40]

Numbers of child-free adults are on the rise. Figures show that nearly one in five women in England and Wales in their late forties have no children—compared to one in ten of their mothers' generation.[41]

having to "do adulting." Badges of rebellion that used to signify youth are now the preserve of the middle-aged. A survey suggested that almost a quarter of forty- to fifty-nine-year-olds have a tattoo somewhere on their body, compared with under one in six of eighteen- to twenty-four-year-olds. They don't want to grow up and settle down, and even if they did, they can't afford to.

So midlife is no longer about "settling down." And older age is not about slowing down, either.

My dad is eighty-one, an accountant, and works a four-day week. My mother is running a café at seventy-six. Both of them are relentless hard workers. Neither of them believes in retirement, which they equate with cardigans, golf, and the slow path to death. They barely believe in weekends. They are part of the zeitgeist. Today, the retirement age is increasing, people are working for longer, and they don't appear to be slowing down.

~~~~~~~~~~

RETHINKING RETIREMENT

In the UK in 1948, the basic state pension age was sixty-five for men and sixty for women. Which made sense; at the time, life expectancy was sixty-six for men and seventy for women.

Life expectancy is much higher today, and pension costs are spiraling. The UK government is increasing the age at which you can claim a state pension to sixty-six from 2020, and the plan is to raise it to sixty-seven by 2028. In addition to this, Office for National Statistics figures show that since 1992, the number of people working beyond sixty-four years of age in the UK has doubled, and more than half of people aged seventy and over who are still working are self-employed.[42]

Boomers who have paid off their mortgages and have decent retirement savings want to spend their money on experiences, for example traveling internationally and going on adventure holidays. And it's not just leisure—they are starting businesses too.

They are also divorcing, finding love in later life, and staying sexually active. In fact, incidents of sexually transmitted infections among the over-sixties have increased—so much so that PornHub, the online pornography platform, has released a sex-ed campaign aimed at the elderly (and they are giving away VHS copies or DVDs to those who are less internet savvy).

Believe the stats, and you paint a picture of a seventy-year-old sexually active entrepreneur with wanderlust. Not someone playing golf in a cardigan.

So these are the demographic and cultural changes that are flexing our life paths. At the same time, the march of technology is creating new futures: of work, of education, of how we live our lives.

ARTIFICIAL INTELLIGENCE
& WHAT IT *REALLY* MEANS
TO BE HUMAN

The World Economic Forum calls today's technological changes the "Fourth Industrial Revolution": life-changing breakthroughs in artificial intelligence, robotics, autonomous vehicles, and 3D printing.

These are incredible leaps forward and will improve our lives in many ways, yet they make us uneasy. A deep anxiety of our time is whether artificial intelligence will not only take our jobs but also make us redundant as humans.

In 2018, Sundar Pichai, CEO of Google, got up in front of the company's annual developer conference, held in Mountain View, California. Live on stage, he demonstrated how their artificial intelligence system, Google Assistant, could book a haircut. The tech community was blown away. It wasn't the task itself; we expect AI to start shouldering some of our dull, everyday tasks. What was jaw-dropping was how Google Assistant did it. The bot made a phone call to the hair salon, with a voice pattern so human, complete with "mm-hmms," pauses, and chitchat, that the receptionist at the salon had no idea she was talking to a robot. If she had, would she have questioned whether that robot was coming after her own job?

For some of us, it might be sooner rather than later.

Google's Ray Kurzweil—a man Bill Gates calls "the best person I know at predicting the future of artificial intelligence"—believes that humans will be outpaced by machines in 2029. That is, in 2029, the first computer will pass the Turing test, where the intelligence of the computer is indistinguishable from that of a human. By then, it is expected that artificial intelligence machines will be part of a company's board of directors. Perhaps it's most sensible to think of AI as our future coworker: So, how will we work alongside it? How can we complement each other? What specific skills will we—as humans—bring to the party?

That last question is the killer. We need to reflect harder on what we humans are for, and what we are good at.

I believe one of the most urgent questions for my daughters' generation is not "What do you want to be when you grow up?" but "What is it, *really*, to be human today?"

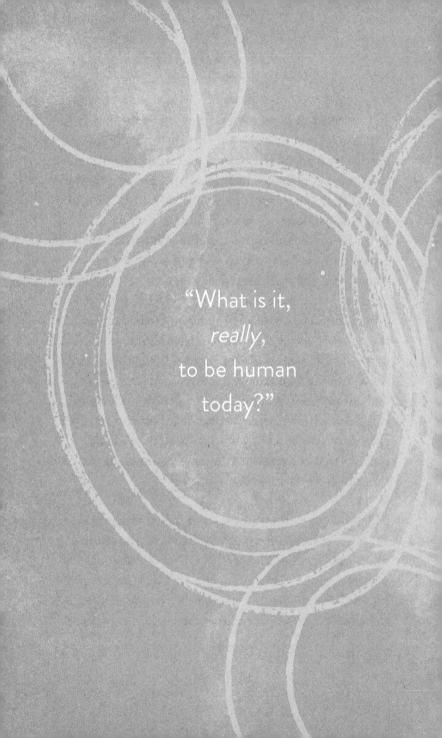

"What is it,
really,
to be human
today?"

In the workplace, we are rewarded for being able to perform like machines—long hours, productivity, efficiency. And this has leaked over into our private lives. We have allowed technology to chip away at the things that matter most to us. Sherry Turkle, clinical psychologist and sociologist at the Massachusetts Institute of Technology, worries how much we are voluntarily sacrificing at the altar of tech. She has shown that the mere presence of an iPhone on the table between two people makes them feel less connected and reduces the quality of their conversation. Even if it's turned facedown. We will have a more shallow conversation, we will skirt over the things that matter, we will fail to look each other in the eyes, empathize, and connect. It's as though the device looms large, still controlling us, a black hole of distraction and intimacy, even as it sits innocently with its back to us. Turkle believes that conversation, that most human of pastimes, is becoming endangered.

My phone already creates stock responses to emails I receive. If someone sends me an article, the phone offers me "Thanks, I'll check it out" or "Looks great!" as possible replies. Can you imagine if I succumbed and hit send and the person on the other end replied with the stock phrases her phone threw out? Our devices would be stuck in a loop of phatic, emotionless, nonsense conversations. It would be funny if it wasn't so depressing.

At the very point we should be nurturing our humanity as the thing that distinguishes us from AI, we are shedding it.

Bots are becoming more human-ish, and humans are becoming more robotic. It makes me think of the ending of George Orwell's *Animal Farm*: "The creatures outside looked from pig to man, and from man to pig, and from pig to man again; but already it was impossible to say which was which."

We're in a crucial moment in time. The pace of change is scorchingly fast compared to the past. Instead of racing to keep up, are we making the time to adjust, contemplate, and be more intentional about our relationship with technology? Technology creeps up on us and makes itself at home, but we need to ask ourselves if it's really welcome.

HOW TO BE HUMAN IN A TECH-DRIVEN WORLD

Step away from your phone at key points in your day. There are whole books dedicated to helping us manage our relationship with technology addiction, but these are the things that have worked for me:

~ Don't charge your phone in your bedroom. Charge it in another room and buy an alarm clock.
~ Don't check your emails within an hour of waking up—otherwise you start the day responding to someone else's agenda rather than your own.
~ Put your phone in another room when you are with your family. A parent staring at their phone as a child tries to get eye contact is a common scenario. Try your hardest to avoid it.
~ Speak honestly and from the heart and avoid using buzzwords, jargon, or stock phrases spewed out by your device. Many thanks!
~ Meet people face-to-face. Chat, look them in the eye, listen; don't just talk at people. Form rapport.
~ Be generous. Share ideas, do favors, introduce people.

HOW TO FLEX
YOUR FUTURE

So what should we be doing? With longer working lives, uncertain life paths, and the unsettling rise of AI, the only thing we can be sure of is that we will need to flex, adapt, and cope with change. What skills should we develop for more fulfilled, longer-lasting working lives?

1. **Learn *how* to learn**
For so long we've seen education as what we learn. A drip feed of information from teacher brain to student brain. Rote learning and testing happen along the way to check the info transaction is working. At some point, we take our info-full brains to the workplace and start spending this knowledge in return for money.

Except this doesn't work. The information kids get today floods them from all directions, not just from their teachers' brains. We need to teach them to interrogate the information they receive, to look at it critically. We need "Post-Truth" lessons in school. This will help children make sense of many conflicting shards of information, determine what to trust and what to dismiss, to find diverse voices rather than merely listening to the status quo, and to use this jigsaw to create a knowledgeable view on a topic.

But it's not just about turning a deluge of information into knowledge. We need to stop simply thinking about *what* we learn and start paying more attention to *how* we learn. In other words, help our kids relearn how to learn. The knowledge they get from school and higher education will not be timeless and resilient to the pace of economic change—especially when the jobs we're training them for may not exist.

In the future, our ability to learn will be valued higher than what we already know. Our children need to leave school with the tools for "learning in the moment" that they can use again and again as they pivot and flex through their careers.

This is the skill of coping with change, of being able to learn new things and leave old assumptions behind.

As Heather E. McGowan, an expert in the future of work, put it, "Having an agile learning mindset will be the new skill set of the twenty-first century."[43]

2. **Check in with yourself every seven years**
A life span of 100 years is daunting and overwhelming. Avivah Wittenberg-Cox, gender expert and author of *Late Love: Mating in Maturity*, recommends breaking it down into seven-year blocks. Every seven years the body replaces itself with a largely new set of cells. Supposedly, the seven-year itch arrives in relationships. At the end of each block, we should take time out to contemplate, assess, and plan (ideally with friends who are going through the same transitions—see point 4 on page 172).

You might ask yourself the following questions:

~ What have I learned from the last seven years?
~ Do I still value the same things?
~ What should I leave behind?
~ What do I need to learn next?
~ Do I want to pivot and change something?

I found these questions really useful when we launched Starling. Adam and I wanted to leave behind the idea of business growth as aggressive targets and hiring more and more people. We wanted to think differently: growth with purpose, horizontal growth that stretched our boundaries, growth in our relationships with our clients.

I wanted to pivot toward a work life characterized by generosity—of time, ideas, and conversations. And generosity with our colleagues to make sure we all had whatever we needed to work best and happiest—and very often this is flexibility.

It really helped to be intentional about this when we started our business. As Wittenberg-Cox says, "You figure out life in the rearview mirror—it doesn't make sense when you are actually going through it. Why do we tend to take the time to contemplate when it's too late? Better to do it earlier."

Some of this involves coming to grips with how to leave behind what is no longer right, useful, or relevant. Like a snake shedding the skin that no longer fits, we need to identify and shed the skills, practices, and opinions that no longer serve us.

3. Reskill, pivot, side-hustle

Change jobs or start side hustles. This is a difficult choice, no matter how much soul-searching you have done. It's hard to move on from a stable job; it's unnerving to swap directions. It's especially difficult for older people—the adult brain is less flexible than the teenage brain, which is primed for change and novelty.

So how can we navigate our own reinvention? One way is to borrow from the Japanese concept of *ikigai* or "a reason for being." The model, designed in a beautiful intersecting diagram, asks the following four questions:

~ What do I love?
~ What am I good at?
~ What can I be paid for now? (Or could this become a future side hustle?)
~ What does the world need?

It's a useful set of questions to help us work out what we really value in our lives, where our skills lie, and what we want to prioritize going forward. It can help us decide where to pivot or what hustle to pursue.

Writing this book is my side hustle. I'm good at coming up with ideas. I love writing. I believe the world needs flex. *Ikigai* would tell me to go for it.

As a result of all this introspection, we'll see older people going back to school and getting undergraduate degrees, or retraining in new industries and starting at the bottom rung again.

A great example of this is Now Teach, a scheme set up by former *Financial Times* journalist Lucy Kellaway, which targets disillusioned and burned-out professionals approaching retirement age and helps them pivot into teaching.

"For me, this had been a long time coming," she says. "When my mom died, I thought I'd had it with journalism because it was too shallow. . . . I sat around with all these journalists fussing over what the headline was, and I thought: 'No, I don't want to do this anymore. I want to do something useful.'"

TIMOTHY PHILLIPS'S FLEX STORY

*Timothy Phillips is an author and works for
a government spending watchdog*

It finally happened one afternoon in 2010 when I was on holiday at the seaside. Sitting in a pub garden, discussing how I felt with some of my best friends, I suddenly felt the balance tip, and I knew that when I returned to London I would definitely be applying to go part-time at my salaried job in order to create proper space to pursue my other interest: writing.

I was already a published author, but now, midway through my second book, I had ended up with greatly increased responsibilities in my salaried job, meaning that it was a real struggle to fit everything else in.

I am well aware that, faced with this problem, not everyone can afford to opt for the salary cut. I was very fortunate to be in that position. Even so, I found that I had to overcome powerful stigmas, both social and personal, in order to take the part-time route.

Might I be sidelined in future considerations for promotion, I worried. Wasn't I opting to enter a cul-de-sac in career terms, thereby signaling a lack of ambition and, more fundamentally, a lack of clarity in my life? Rather than focusing on doing one thing well, didn't I run the risk of doing two things badly?

In that pub garden, I suddenly realized that I owed it to myself to give the twin careers approach a try. After all, I was genuinely enjoying both my jobs and I knew that each of them satisfied different needs and provided me with fulfillment in different ways.

I am glad to say that I have never regretted my decision. My second book was published in 2017, and I am now planning a third. I got back some of the free time I had previously lost through being too busy and have used it to do the things that people need to do in order to relax and recuperate: to enjoy my family, to exercise, to read for pleasure.

Even in the part of my life where I was prepared to take a hit, I have been surprised to find that my bosses have not overlooked me for promotion, and also that they have respected my contracted hours. As so many professionals who go part-time say, I have definitely learned to work more efficiently than in the past and I now find it easier to be decisive in the workplace and to empower my teams through delegation and by trusting them more.

I think I originally suspected that, someday, one of my two careers would end up taking the lead again and that I would leave the other one behind. But now I'm not so sure. I feel that the two together help me to achieve an equilibrium in my life in a way that neither on its own could supply.

So Kellaway set up Now Teach for older people who want to spend their energy and time doing something meaningful. One thousand people applied and were whittled down to the first cohort of forty-five. Kellaway is now a math teacher in east London and finds it "exhilarating, alien, exciting, exhausting. I'm mentally pinching myself every minute of the day thinking, 'Am I really a teacher?' "[44]

4. Love your friends

We are living longer and going through more ups, downs, and transitions along the way. We can share some of our emotional decision-making with partners and family members, but it's still a lot to take on. We need friendships more than ever to sustain and inspire us. Long-running studies have shown that people who have quality, warm friendships in their lives are healthier, happier, and live longer.

We have neglected our friends, though. Philosopher Alain de Botton wrote: "A good set of friends can be the making of a really good life. But it's just very, very hard to find. We are obsessed by our careers and by our love life. Friendships come very much third, particularly when people start to have children—friends really go out the window then."[45]

THE GLOBAL LONELINESS EPIDEMIC

According to the Office for National Statistics, in 2016 to 2017, 5 percent of people over sixteen—or one in twenty adults—in England reported feeling lonely often or always.[46] According to a 2018 Ipsos survey of 20,000 US adults, nearly half of Americans report sometimes or always feeling alone or left out.[47]

In South Korea, single-person households constitute more than a quarter of all households in the country. Loneliness in South Korea has even spawned a new subculture called *honjok*—a term that loosely means "loners," combining *hon* (alone) and *jok* (tribe).

We need friends, but we've forgotten how to do friendship.

Okinawa in Japan is one of the world's "Blue Zones" (regions of the world where people live much longer than average). There, people form a social network called a *moai*. Traditionally, when a child is born, they are put into a group with four other children born around the same time. This is their *moai*, a lifelong crew. Together they support one another—emotionally, socially,

even financially—over a lifetime, meeting regularly to exchange news and gossip and offer advice.

I like the idea of the *moai*. But you can't just snap your fingers and get a ready-made *moai*. Studies say two people need to spend 90 hours together to become friends, or 200 hours to qualify as close friends. Clearly we need to invest time and energy in our friendships.

But how? Instead of digging into academic studies to determine the rules of sustaining enriching friendships, I decided to take my own advice and act more like a human. I asked my own friends. Here's what they said:

1. **Have interweaving lives**. Know and care about each other's friends and families. One friend is an advocate of the "minestrone," a dinner party deliberately mixing people from different parts of your life into one big friend soup. She says this means your friendships deepen, because there are more cross-connections. But it also shows you for who you are in your entirety, rather than fragmenting yourself for different types of friends.

2. **Have shared experiences** (like weekends away, dinners, hanging out and watching MTV) rather than just snatched coffees to catch up on separate lives. A few friends criticize the "catch-up coffee," saying it shouldn't be the only way you interact. It relies too much on the past and the frantic present. It doesn't invest you in the future of your relationship. Unlike point 3 . . .

3. **Have parties!** Parties make new stories and memories. They mark milestones, they celebrate being alive, and they involve dancing. The best ones have conga lines.

4. **Ask for help**; don't just present a polished, Instagrammable, perfect life to each other. Help can be as small as asking a friend to do the school run, or as big as asking for support when you are going through a sad time. It doesn't just benefit you. People like being asked for help.

5. **But don't be a "friend parasite."** We all have that friend who habitually offloads their problems in energy-sapping monologues, without asking a single question in return. Each encounter with the "friend parasite" leaves you feeling drained and a bit diminished.

6. **Be generous about changing circumstances.** Allow friendships to flex and evolve. Don't hold your friends hostage to the people they were when you met.

7. **Be kind.** Don't demand every meet-up is exciting and fun. Allow each other to be tired and fed up sometimes.

8. **Be tolerant.** Don't judge them too much, or hold them to impossible standards. A friend's grandpa always said: "You've got to shut one eye to make a friend and both eyes to keep them."

9. **Have a range of friends:** don't expect the world from any one person.

SUMMARY

My eighty-one-year-old accountant dad hates computers. It's clear the robots are coming for a big slice of his job. Number crunching, analysis, spreadsheets—all of these will be done by something like Google Assistant that was so good at booking a haircut.

But he has future-proofed himself because his clients love him for his humanity, his empathy, his complex problem-solving. These are exactly the qualities that machines will never be able to rival. Listening to someone going through a transition like divorce or death of a loved one and helping them work out what to do next is at the heart of the human experience in these changing times. Being a friend and having friends staves off sadness and ill health. The skills of friendship can reduce the likelihood of a robot taking your job.

We need to be able to show sensitivity and compassion to ourselves—whether it is every seven years, as advocated by Wittenberg-Cox, or at regular points with our version of a *moai*, throughout our increasingly zigzagging journey through life. This will help us pivot, adapt, and evolve as the world around us changes. Because the ability to flex to change will be a superpower. As futurist and philosopher Alvin Toffler said, "The illiterate of the twenty-first century will not be those who cannot read and write, but those who cannot learn, unlearn, and relearn."

AFTER WORD

In this book, I've looked at flex across different areas of our lives—creativity and flexibility of thinking; work and the nine-to-five; home, relationships, and the emotional load; our body and its rhythms and cycles; and finally, our futures.

Thinking flexibly in all of these areas has changed my life. But it hasn't always been easy. There was the three-day working week that turned into a shitshow; the years of tiredness and forcing myself to be productive before I understood my body's rhythms and cycles; the endless meetings and screen time that stifled creative thought. Since I have learned how to flex, I have found the confidence to face up to challenges and apparent impasses with a bravery and inventiveness I couldn't have mustered before.

At first glance, the word "flexibility" may appear to describe something that is soft or pliable. Flexible people might seem like pushovers, bending over backward to fit in, marching to someone else's drum. But I hope I have shown here that flex gives us power; to flex is to show immense strength.

It does not mean succumbing to the ever-increasing demands on our time and attention. Done right, on our own terms, it gives us resilience to our toxic culture of presenteeism, time pressure, and ultimately burnout. It helps us escape the army of octopus lady jugglers, crazed with the exhaustion of "having it all." It allows us to live longer lives more sustainably. It gives us self-worth—which brings with it the ability to say no when something doesn't work for us, and yes when it does. And as much as we want to own our own time, we don't want to do all of this alone. We want to work out how to flex with the people who are most precious to us.

Flex doesn't mean messy. When done right, flex has sharp edges. Flex embodies the definitive decisions we make when circumstances change, and the precise limits of our own energy and capacity. It is the boundaries we put in place to protect us, such as new lines drawn in the home to share the load and share the joy. Flex is the space we make for our own creativity, which intensifies it and makes it thrive and flourish.

Flex is brave. It takes chutzpah to challenge society's norms and the structures that surround us. To break our way out of echo chambers. To call out what's wrong and invent new solutions. Perhaps the bravest thing of all is not knowing all the answers but having the courage to experiment, to invent, to make things up as we go.

Because, when you boil it all down, flex is about asking ourselves one big question: How do I want to live this beautiful life? And then going out there and doing it.

REFERENCES

1 Rothman, Joshua, "Creativity Creep," *New Yorker*, September 2, 2014.

2 Asimov, Isaac, "On Creativity," *Technology Review*, January/February 2015.

3 From a study conducted by researchers at the University of California, San Diego; see Bilton, Nick, "Part of the Daily American Diet, 34 Gigabytes of Data," New York Times, December 9, 2009, www.nytimes .com/2009/12/10/technology/10data .html.

4 Mark, Gloria, et al., "The Cost of Interrupted Work: More Speed and Stress," 2008, www.ics.uci.edu/~gmark/chi08 -mark.pdf.

5 Tadmor, Carmit T., et al., "Not Just for Stereotyping Anymore: Racial Essentialism Reduces Domain-General Creativity," *Psychological Science*, Vol. 24, Iss. 1, January 2013.

6 Gross, Jessica, "Walking Meetings? 5 Surprising Thinkers Who Swore by Them," April 29, 2013, blog.ted.com /walking-meetings-5-surprising-thinkers -who-swore-by-them/.

7 Oppezzo, Maria, and Schwartz, Daniel L., "Give Your Ideas Some Legs: The Positive Effect of Walking on Creative Thinking," 2014, www.apa.org/pubs /journals/releases/xlm-a0036577.pdf.

8 Burkemann, Oliver, "Interview: Jerry Seinfeld on How to Be Funny Without Sex and Swearing," *Guardian*, January 5, 2014, www.theguardian.com/culture/2014/jan /05/jerry-seinfeld-funny-sex-swearing -sitcom-comedy.

9 Dave Chappelle to Jerry Seinfeld, *Comedians in Cars Getting Coffee*, Season 10, July 2018.

10 "International Comparisons of UK Productivity (ICP), Final Estimates: 2015," April 5, 2017, www.ons.gov.uk/economy /economicoutputandproductivity /productivitymeasures/bulletins /internationalcomparisonsofproductivity finalestimates/2015.

11 "Presenteeism Hits Record High in UK Organisations as Stress at Work Rises," May 2, 2018, www.cipd.co.uk/about/media /press/020518-health-wellbeing-survey.

12 "Employees Spend 2.5 Weeks a Year Working When Ill—Costing Businesses £4k per Employee in Lost Productivity," October 13, 2017, www.ntu.ac.uk/about-us /news/news-articles/2017/10/employees

-spend-2.5-weeks-a-year-working-when-ill
-costing-businesses-4k-per-employee-in-lost
-productivity.

13 Whelan, Pam, "CIPD Health and
Well-Being at Work Report—2018," May 2,
2018, insights.simplyhealth.co.uk/insights
/cipd-health-and-well-being-at-work-report
-2018.

14 From a poll of 2,000 adults undertaken
as part of research by the charity Mental
Health UK, d1wk4hs734fd0n.cloudfront
.net/assets/genesis/landing_pages/MHAW
/eve_mattress_infographic_final.png.

15 "The Future Is Flexible: The Importance
of Flexibility in the Modern Workplace,"
www.werk.co/research.

16 Rogers, Charlotte, "Salary Survey
2018: Wellbeing and the Future of Work,"
January 11, 2018, www.marketingweek
.com/2018/01/11/salary-survey-2018
-wellbeing-and-the-future-of-work/.

17 Stepler, Renee, "5 Facts About Family
Caregivers," November 18, 2015, www
.pewresearch.org/fact-tank/2015/11/18
/5-facts-about-family-caregivers/.

18 *Flexible Working Provision and Uptake*,
May 2012, www.ask4flex.org/UK-_Flexible
_Working_Survey_Report--CIPD.pdf.

19 "The Future Is Flexible: The Importance
of Flexibility in the Modern Workplace,"
werk.co/documents/The
%20Future%20is%20Flexible%20-%20
Werk%20Flexibility%20Study.pdf.

20 Lynch, Shana, "Why Working from
Home Is a 'Future-Looking Technology,'"
June 22, 2017, www.gsb.stanford.edu/
insights/why-working-home-future
-looking-technology.

21 "Deloitte Survey: Less Than Half of
People Surveyed Feel Their Organization
Helps Men Feel Comfortable Taking
Parental Leave," June 15, 2016, www
.prnewswire.com/news-releases/deloitte
-survey-less-than-half-of-people-surveyed
-feel-their-organization-helps-men-feel
-comfortable-taking-parental-leave-3002
84822.html.

22 Schofield, Hugh, "The Plan to Ban
Work Emails Out of Hours," May 11,
2016, www.bbc.co.uk/news/magazine
-36249647.

23 Slaughter, Anne-Marie, "Why Women
Still Can't Have It All," *Atlantic*, July/
August 2012.

24 Ortiz-Espina, Esteban, and Tzvetkova,
Sandra, "Working Women: Key Facts and
Trends in Female Labor Force Participation,"
October 16, 2017, www.ourworldindata
.org/female-labor-force-participation
-key-facts.

25 "Women Shoulder the Responsibility
of 'Unpaid Work,'" November 10, 2016,

www.ons.gov.uk/employmentandlabour
market/peopleinwork/earningsand
workinghours/articles/womenshoulderthe
responsibilityofunpaidwork/2016-11-10.

26 Westervelt, Amy, "In Japan, the Rise of
the House Husband Redraws Established
Gender Norms," *Post Magazine*, July 2018.

27 Rhodes, Giulia, " 'It Was Like a
Marriage, Only Better': The Single Mothers
Who Moved In Together," *Guardian*,
September 29, 2018.

28 Bauman, Valerie, "Chore Wars:
American Men Are Helping Out More
Around the House—but Women Aren't
Doing Any Less Work as a Result, Data
Says," *Daily Mail*, August 15, 2018.

29 Khazan, Olga, "Emasculated Men
Refuse to Do Chores—Except Cooking,"
Atlantic, October 24, 2016.

30 "Not All Housework Is Created Equal:
Particular Housework Tasks and Couples'
Relationship Quality," April 3, 2016,
www.contemporaryfamilies.org/house
workandrelationshipquality/.

31 "Men Enjoy Five Hours More Leisure
Time per Week Than Women," January 9,
2018, www.ons.gov.uk/peoplepopulation
andcommunity/wellbeing/articles/men
enjoyfivehoursmoreleisuretimeperweek
thanwomen/2018-01-09.

32 Brewer, Gayle, and Hendrie, Colin A.,
"Evidence to Suggest That Copulatory
Vocalizations in Women Are Not a
Reflexive Consequence of Orgasm,"
Archives of Sexual Behavior, Vol. 40,
Iss. June 3, 2011.

33 "Mumsnet's Justine Roberts: I Made
a List of All Our Jobs on a Spreadsheet. I
Had 65 and My Husband Had Five," *Daily
Standard*, May 30, 2013, www.standard
.co.uk/lifestyle/london-life/mumsnets
-justine-roberts-i-made-a-list-of-all-our
-jobs-on-a-spreadsheet-i-had-65-and-my
-husband-had-8637312.html.

34 "Same- and Different-Sex Couples
Negotiating at Home," www.familiesand
work.org/downloads/modern-families.pdf.

35 Read, Erin, "Whether a Husband
Identifies as a Breadwinner Depends on
Whether He Respects His Wife's Career—
Not on How Much She Earns," *Harvard
Business Review*, August 15,2018.

36 Suni, Eric, "Teens and Sleep," August 5,
2020, See www.sleepfoundation.org/sleep
-topics/teens-and-sleep.

37 Lyttleton, Ben, *Edge: Leadership
Secrets from Football's Top Thinkers*,
HarperCollins, 2017.

38 Frey, Carl Benedikt, and Osborne,
Michael A., "The Future of Employment:
How Susceptible Are Jobs to Computerisa-
tion?," September 17, 2013, www.oxford
martin.ox.ac.uk/downloads/academic/The
_Future_of_Employment.pdf.

39 *The Side Hustle Economy*, July 2018,
assets.henley.ac.uk/defaultUploads/PDFs

/news/Journalists-Regatta-Henley
_Business_School_whitepaper_DIGITAL
.pdf?mtime=20180703154430&_ga=2
.120242955.240996529.1532257388
-827778871.1532257388.

40 Kollewe, Julia, "Quarter of Households
in UK Will Rent Privately by End of 2021,
Says Report," *Guardian*, June 12, 2017.

41 "Childbearing for Women Born in
Different Years, England and Wales: 2016,"
November 24, 2017, www.ons.gov.uk
/peoplepopulationandcommunity/births
deathsandmarriages/conception and
fertilityrates/bulletins/childbearing for
womenbornindifferentyearsenglandand
wales/2016.

42 Jones, Dan, "Gig Economy: Time to
Shift the Spotlight to Older Self-Employed
Workers," October 3, 2017, www.ageing
-better.org.uk/news/gig-economy-time-shift
-spotlight-older-self-employed-workers.

43 Friedman, Thomas L., "An Agile
Learning Mindset Is the Only Way You'll
Own Your Own Future," *Seattle Times*, May
11, 2017, www.seattletimes.com/opinion
/an-agile-learning-mindset-is-the-only
-way-youll-own-your-own-future/.

44 O'Kelly, Lisa, " 'I'm Getting a Big Buzz
out of It': Five Former Professionals on Their
First Term Teaching," *Guardian*, March 11,
2018, www.theguardian.com/education
/2018/mar/11/im-getting-a-big-buzz
-former-professionals-teaching-lucy
-kellaway-now-teach.

45 Stuart, Julia, "The Strange Case of
the Death of Friendship," *Independent*,
November 7, 2001, www.independent.co
.uk/arts-entertainment/books/news
/the-strange-case-death-friendship
-9137637.html.

46 "Loneliness—What Characteristics and
Circumstances Are Associated with Feeling
Lonely?," April 10, 2018, www.ons.gov.uk
/peoplepopulationandcommunity/
wellbeing/articles/lonelinesswhat
characteristicsandcircumstancesare
associatedwithfeelinglonely/2018-04-10.

47 "Cigna's US Loneliness Index: Survey
of 20,000 Americans Examining Behaviors
Driving Loneliness in the United States,"
May 1, 2018, www.multivu.com/players
/English/8294451-cigna-us-loneliness
-survey/.

ACKNOWLEDGMENTS

Thank you to the dear friends and family who waded through early drafts: Andy, Robert, Pauline, and Daniel Auerbach, Andrea Lyttleton, Katie Churcher, Marina Camiletti, Jenny and David Silverman, Adam Chmielowski, Annie Crombie, Tammy Reynolds, and especially Ben Lyttleton.

Thanks to the friends and expert colleagues whose ears I bent (flexed) and who gave me such interesting perspectives: Anthony Bale, Zoe Bloom, Daisy Donovan, Helen Dwyer, Sarah Galgey, Annie Gallimore, Cindy Gallop, Emma Gannon, Pinny Grylls, Sarah Hesz, Katharine Hill, Jules McKeen, Timothy Phillips, Miriam Rayman, Kate Shepherd Cohen, Anniki Sommerville, Dale Southerton, Jan Toledano, Amelia Torode, Mark Williamson, Avivah Wittenberg-Cox, and Rosie and Faris Yakob.

And huge thanks to the amazingly talented team at HQ: Lisa Milton, Kate Fox, Joe Thomas, Liz Marvin, Jen Callahan Packer, Noleen Robinson, Jo Surman, and Charlie Redmayne.

My gratitude also to the brilliant US team at HarperOne: Anna Paustenbach, Judith Curr, Melinda Mullin, Maxwell Shanley, Lucile Culver, Makenna Holford, and Mary Grangeia—thank you!

ABOUT THE AUTHOR

ANNIE AUERBACH is a speaker, consultant, author, and cofounder of the trends agency Starling, which specializes in keeping brands relevant through understanding cultural change. She has worked flexibly for twenty years throughout her career—part-time, remote working, freelancing, through a portfolio career, and returning to work after having her two daughters.